EMMA WOOD was born in
History at Cambridge Univ
running a junk stall on local
Highlands and wrote *Note*
Hydro Boys (2002). She ha

By the same author:

Notes from the North, Luath Press, 1998
The Hydro Boys, Luath Press, 2002

Peatbogs, Plague and Potatoes

How climate change and geology shaped Scotland's history

EMMA WOOD

Luath Press Limited

EDINBURGH

www.luath.co.uk

First published 2009

ISBN: 978-1-906307-37-0

The author's right to be identified as author of this book
under the Copyright, Designs and Patents Act 1988 has been asserted.

The paper used in this book is recyclable.
It is made from low chlorine pulps produced in a low energy,
low emissions manner from renewable forests.

The publisher acknowledges subsidy from

Scottish
Arts Council

towards the publication of this volume.

Printed and bound by Bell & Bain Ltd., Glasgow

Typeset in 10.5 point Sabon

Acknowledgements

I respectfully and gratefully acknowledge my debt to the authors listed in the Bibliography; as his extensive citation suggests, the work of Professor TC Smout has been of great influence and assistance. Thanks also to the many individuals who have provided information, inspiration and invaluable assistance, including Tim O'Riordan, Andrew MacLeman, Bob Powell, Bob Sim, Chrissie Hewlett, Dingwall Library, Dorothy Burr, Ernie Dan Mackenzie, Fiona Robertson, Hector Munro of Foulis, Professor James Hunter, Jasmine Woodcraft, John Huckett, Karen Evans, Lucy Dargue, Marj Donaldson, Marta McGlyn, Merry Hinton, Nancy Kinloch, Sandra and Howie of Wester Laide, Steve Evans, Sue and Christopher Hibbert, Scott Russell, Tom Evans, Truna, Vic Gatrell. The translation of verse by Servasius (© Kenneth Rexroth) which serves as the epigraph to this book is reproduced with the kind permission of the Estate of Kenneth Rexroth.

Contents

For Rod and Beth Harbinson and in fond memory of Ruth Frankenberg, Roddie Bell, Tracey Macleman and Sheila Turner.

Rivers level granite mountains,
Rains wash the figures from the sundial,
The ploughshare wears thin in the furrow;
And on the fingers of the mighty,
The gold of authority is bright
With the glitter of attrition.

(Servasius, 4th century ce,
translated by Kenneth Rexroth)

Preface

CONCERN FOR THE ENVIRONMENT and awareness of the radical and potentially disastrous implications of human impacts on it have intensified dramatically over the years I have been writing this book. *Peatbogs, Plague and Potatoes* takes as its subject the environmental history of Scotland, from the very beginning to 1860 when, with the demise of subsistence farming, the country's economy became fully modernised. The largely preindustrial period under examination offers much illumination as to the significance of the non-human environment for human existence. It also provides a context for understanding the complex environmental challenges we continue to face. Climate change is not a new phenomenon. In the Bronze Age severe climate change triggered over 2,000 years of heavy rainfall and low temperatures; fertility in the uplands was destroyed and their inhabitants were disadvantaged well into modern times. The harsh conditions of the Little Ice Age, which started in the 14th century and lasted for 500 years, impoverished Scotland's medieval economy and in the 17th century prompted the country's first waves of economic migration.

For our preindustrial ancestors, environmental disaster was

either a powerful memory or, as Burns the ploughman knew only too well, the cause of future dread. Only a dozen or so human generations have passed since climate change last caused starvation to paralyse Scotland. The technical proficiency achieved in the intervening years must now be devoted to preparing for – if not averting – disruption and here historical awareness has a role to play.

Conventional history tends to neglect the environmental perspective, and with it the information which might enable us to deal with climate change in the 21st century and beyond. This book, through a Scottish focus, demonstrates the power of the environment to shape human experience. It also provides tools of understanding relevant to issues which transcend nationality.

Starting Points

ENVIRONMENTAL HISTORY PLACES factors such as climate change, soil formation, pollution and farming at the forefront of its explanation of events in the past, in contrast with conventional history's preoccupation with human struggles for power and profit. In that incomplete version of events, nature is seen as a neutral backdrop to human affairs, a resource to be plundered or a hostile element to be tamed. Animals and the weather have exerted profound influences over humanity, but unless it's stormy on the day of a battle or a wild animal bites a human bigwig, conventional history does not acknowledge this connection, or the respect for the non-human environment it inspires. Supposedly comprehensive accounts of agricultural modernisation focus more on increased yields than on reduced biodiversity. Descriptions of industrialisation tend to ignore the pollution it produced.

The myriad connections and interactions which make up environmental history are usually divided into the environment's impact on humans, human impact on the environment, and cultural attitudes towards the environment. I have concentrated on the first two classes because material such as Gaelic poetry or Enlightenment philosophy, is much more accessible than the dispersed and disparate evidence of interactions between human and non-human elements of the Scottish environment; and also because recording attitudes to the non-human environment only replicates the human-centredness of conventional history. Yet it is the case that what humans write, think or say about the environment is often less informative for the environmental historian than records of what they actually do to the environment. Sources such as pollen analysis and records from the grain, timber and fur trades are more directly revealing of environmental realities than any amount of poems or sermons.

The definition of 'environmental' given in the *Oxford English Dictionary* – relating to the natural world and the impact of human activity on its condition – implies that humans are less 'natural' than other inhabitants of the planet. What exactly is meant by the 'natural world'? Scotland's landscape is often referred to as natural, mainly because of its relative emptiness. However, hardly anything in Scotland's environment is as it was when the first people arrived.

In the second half of the 20th century, to try to resolve difficult and important questions about the environment and humans' place within it, a new spectrum of ethics was devised to extend the scope of moral significance beyond human beings to non-human elements of the environment. Biocentric and ecocentric ethics challenge the anthropocentric attitudes that have held sway in the West since Plato and Aristotle and which are powerfully present in the Judaeo-Christian tradition – hence the concentration in conventional history on human activities and concerns. The promotion of human over non-human interests was first rationalised and refined by Francis Bacon (1561–1626), who declared that 'the whole world works together in the service of man; and there is nothing from which he does not derive use and fruit'. He urged 'enlarging the bounds of the human empire to the effecting of all things possible', sentiments that triumphed in the 18th century with the Enlightenment. Scots thinkers including David Hume and Adam Smith were at the forefront of this intellectual revolution which stressed the primacy of humankind's social and economic interests, and championed freedom of thought and of economic opportunity. The enduring belief in the primacy of humanity's social and economic interests lies behind many current environmental crises.

The ethic informing this environmental history is what the new classification defines as weakly anthropocentric – a version of environmentalism that acknowledges the material, spiritual, pragmatic and respectful obligations of humans to the non-human environment. The deep ecological positions that see humanity as just another planetary species with no special rights over the Earth or its other inhabitants make useful correctives to influential anthropocentric assumptions. But rather than imagining away human populations, however advantageous that might be for the non-human environment, I will concentrate on humankind's relations with that non-human environment.

In compiling this narrative, I have used information about environmental trends gathered from a variety of conventional histories. The resulting broad-brush treatment of this extensive subject makes omissions inevitable but it does demonstrate the issues which underlie environmental history. This history starts at the very beginning of the lands now called Scotland. It ends with the passing of subsistence agriculture there, as signalled by the beginnings of industrialisation and by the country's last famines. The end of peasant farming happened differently in different parts of the country, and at different times, but very little traditional farming survived anywhere in Scotland after the 1850s.

I should explain my use of the word 'Scotland'. I mean to discuss the environmental history of the lands we know as Scotland today. These lands did not constitute a single, entire, national territory until the 15th century; until as late as the 9th century 'Scotland' meant only a part of that territory. The name was derived from the Scots, a Celtic tribe who came from Dalriada in Northern Ireland before the 4th century ce, settling in what is now Argyll in significant numbers during the following 200 years. Not until the 15th century did 'Scotland' signify the extent of territory that it does today; the Lothians and Strathclyde as well as the Northern and Western Isles have not always been parts of the Scottish state.

In fact, the name's Anglian suffix means it was probably coined by enemy Angle populations in Northumbria and the Lothians after *c*.800 ce. But to use geomorphic terms like the Southern Uplands or political ones like Northern Britain to describe the country and its constituent parts in former times would be artificial and unacceptable respectively. To make up for using 'Scotland' to describe a geographical entity without reference to changing political realities, I have included a chronology of those changes showing the development of the Scottish state.

'Lowlands' also requires definition: capitalised, it is used to refer to all of Scotland south of the Highland Boundary Fault, despite the fact that this area contains significant elevated portions of land; lower-case 'lowlands' is a general term for land areas at elevations less than 400m above sea level.

Dates in the Christian Era are indicated 'ce' up to 1000; 'bp' means before present.

PART ONE

Prehistory

I

The Very Beginning

THE EARTH DICTATES factors of prime importance for human activity: climate, topography, minerals and soils. Geology is central to the environmental history of Scotland. It defines the different geographical regions of the country and explains how these regions came to be where and what they were when the human population arrived, around 14,000 years ago.

Scotland has a unique diversity of geology and landscape formations for its size, a diversity reflecting the huge age of the land and of the planet itself. The landscape discovered by the first humans was the product of over three billion years of geological evolution featuring erosion and deposition caused by volcanoes, inundations, ice-sheets, wind and rain.

This elemental drama unfolded against a background of continual climate change resulting from another profoundly influential geological process, Continental Drift. This is the gradual movement of continent-sized portions of the Earth's crust across oceans and through different climatic belts. Continental Drift, moving billions of tons of rock up to 10cm each year, is powered by convection currents operating within the Earth and produced by the Earth's hot core. Throughout tens of thousands of millions of years, Continental Drift caused Scotland to occupy many positions around the globe. The mix of tectonic movement, changing climate and volcanic activity experienced by Scotland in her terrestrial wanderings created, and continues to create, key elements of the country's environment.

The oldest rocks in Scotland are found in the northwest mainland and the Outer Hebrides. They originated from volcanic activity around 3,000 million years ago. High temperatures within the Earth's crust then deformed and crystallised these rocks into Lewisian gneiss. About 1,000 million years ago, before the opening of the Atlantic Ocean, they were uplifted in a mountain chain that reached Scotland from Canada and Greenland. Over the next 200 million years, rivers draining the first mountains of Greenland deposited sand and pebbles one kilometre deep onto the gneiss. This layer, of what became known as Torridonian Sandstone, was profoundly eroded over time, leaving only isolated hills like Suilven in Sutherland and Liathach and Ben Alligin on Loch Torridon in Wester Ross.

Around 440 million years ago, the physical composition and positioning of the Earth's continental landmasses differed completely from today. The land areas now known as Scotland and England were in the southern hemisphere located in separate continents on opposite sides of the Iapetus Ocean, a body of water bigger than the modern North Atlantic. As the Iapetus Ocean began to close up, Scotland and England drifted gradually towards each other. Eventually, the ancient ocean disappeared altogether and the two pieces of land collided.

The scar of this cataclysmic adhesion, the Iapetus Suture, runs under the Earth's crust, just north of Hadrian's Wall. But the gigantic pressures created by this collision also produced more visible effects. They powered a geological event of great magnitude, the Caledonian Orogeny, an episode of mountain-building caused by disturbance in the Earth's crust produced in Scotland's case by tectonic forces, which may have lasted for over a million years. The heat and pressure caused by the Orogeny's crustal collision changed the existing sedimentary rocks of the northern Scottish mainland into schists and quartzites and folded and uplifted them to form the Caledonian Mountains. These peaks stood perhaps as high as the modern Himalayas, from Argyll to the Shetland Islands, part of a new mountain chain that stretched from the Appalachians to western Norway. Scotland's section of the Caledonian Mountains was weathered and eroded over approximately four hundred million years to form the Grampian Mountains that dominate the north of Scotland today.

The Caledonian Orogeny had other effects on the land's evolving shape. One of these was the intrusion of molten rock through the Earth's crust that cooled to form granite and other related rocks such as gabbro and pegmatite. More resistant to weathering and erosion than adjacent metamorphic rocks, granite forms some of the most substantial mountains in Scotland, including Ben Nevis, at 1,344m the highest Scottish peak. Granite has an iconic importance in the country's landscape, present, for example, at Peterhead and the Cairngorm massif in the east, Rannoch Moor, Strontian and Mull in the west and in Galloway in the southwest.

The Caledonian Orogeny also had important consequences for southern Scotland: here a narrow belt of gently curving hills, the Southern Uplands, was formed from the deep-sea sediments that had accumulated on the floor of the Iapetus Ocean. The forces unleashed by the Caledonian Orogeny lifted these sediments into a series of folds and metamorphosed them into layers of sandstone and shale.

The final legacy of the Caledonian Orogeny shaped the Scottish environment and human experience within it. When the tectonic motion and mountain-building ceased, the Earth's crust came to rest and its smaller pieces joined together along fault lines, many of which are visible in landforms today.

The Highland Boundary Fault and the Southern Upland Fault run parallel east to west from Stonehaven to Arran and form the bounds of a lower rift valley occupying central Scotland, called by geologists the Midland Valley; it consists of a piece of the Earth's crust sunk between these parallel bounding faults.

By between 400 and 360 million years ago, Scotland was between 20 and 10 degrees south of the Equator and experiencing desert conditions. Rivers carried mud and sand off the Caledonian Mountains into the Midland Valley and to the Moray Firth Basin and the Orkneys. The river-borne debris appears in these areas as the rock for which geologists have named this era: Old Red Sandstone. Soils in the Midland Valley derived from Old Red Sandstone are often coloured red by their high iron content. Scotland was also the site of volcanic activity at this time. Its legacy of volcanic rocks includes the Campsie Fells, the Ochils, the Cargunnock Hills, and Castle Rock and Arthur's Seat in Edinburgh.

Scotland continued to drift northwards and by the Carboniferous Period, between 350 and 300 million years ago, had reached northern equatorial latitudes. Tropical rainforests and swamps covered the Midland Valley. Over time, their peaty remains were transformed into coal under the weight of layers of sandstone and shale. These layers were deposited around 260 million years ago as Scotland moved north to arid zones where once again the country experienced desert conditions. Geologists call this era New Red Sandstone. Where sand accumulated in the North Sea Basin, pockets of oil and gas developed, derived respectively from marine plankton remains and buried coal.

Scotland went on moving northwards as part of a super-continent incorporating Greenland and the eastern side of North America. About 65 million years ago, tectonic shifts started to bring the Atlantic Ocean into being. The stretching and thinning of the Earth's crust as the new ocean emerged west of Scotland allowed molten rock to erupt through the crust. This volcanic activity created Iceland, Rockall and the Faeroes. Lava flowed from a line of volcanoes to form a volcanic plateau along Scotland's west coast. Now severely denuded, its remnants form St Kilda, Skye, Rum, Eigg, Staffa, Mull, Arran, the Ardnamurchan peninsula and Ailsa Craig. These are the youngest rocks in Scotland.

Meltdown: Postglacial Climate, Regional Geography and Soils

Climate

The current geological period is the Quaternary: a major geological era that began roughly two million years ago, by which time Scotland was probably not far from her present position on the globe, approximately 57 degrees North and 4 degrees West. Global position, because it determines climate, impacts decisively on every country's environmental history.

Climate, defined as the sum total of long-term weather trends, is the most significant aspect of any region's environment determining the experience of every living thing. Planetary influences such as sunspot activity and the tilt of the Earth's axis affect long-term weather trends including those causing glaciation and deglaciation. But a region's latitude (its distance north or south of the Equator) governs the duration of both day and season; these lengths control the key relationships between the gain and loss of solar energy, the global climate's chief power source.

However, climate is also influenced by local factors such as topography. A significant proportion of Scotland – as much as two thirds – is classified as upland, being at least 300m above sea level. Altitude makes an important difference to climate: temperatures fall as altitude increases with a loss (under standard conditions) of 0.65 degrees Celsius for every 100m increase in altitude.

Heat and moisture, climate's raw materials, are transported by winds and ocean currents. Scotland's location affects the operation of these delivery systems. A potent influence in the evolution of the country's postglacial climate is the Atlantic Ocean. Prevailing southwesterly winds bring moist air from the Atlantic, especially to the west, while the east, more sheltered by high ground, experiences a lower average rainfall.

The Atlantic makes another important contribution that has endured since the end of the country's last glaciation and is crucial to human existence there: the Gulf Stream, which flows north from the Caribbean, past the west coast of Scotland and on to the Orkneys. The warmth of its waters and of the air passing across it means that Scotland (particularly to the west) has a significantly milder climate than other places on the same latitude, like Moscow and Stockholm.

Scotland's postglacial climate can be described broadly as temperate and oceanic, generally wettest and warmest in the west and coldest in the uplands. However, these generalisations do not mean that Scotland's climate has remained the same since the end of the last glaciation. In fact, since its postglacial warming, its pattern has changed constantly, with average temperatures, rainfall and storminess fluctuating over the centuries. The country's global position, climatically influenced by both Europe's continental land mass and the Atlantic Ocean, exposes her to a powerful variety of weather and has resulted in an environmental history that clearly demonstrates the vulnerability of the human population to climate in the preindustrial era.

Palaeoclimatologists have approximately identified and dated the major climatic trends of the Quaternary. Of fundamental importance here are the changes associated with the end of the last major glaciations to occur in Scotland. Glaciation occurs because of regular coolings of the global climate, with summer temperatures throughout the northern hemisphere too low to melt the previous winter's snowfall. Whenever this has occurred over the last two million years, the resulting ice growth caused the development of polar ice caps and the intermittent extension as far as southern Europe of massive land-based ice-sheets, some nearly two and a half miles thick in places.

The last major ice-sheet to affect Scotland began to develop about 30,000 years ago. For most of this last cold episode, Arctic temperatures were the norm, with Scotland's ice cover, centred on Rannoch Moor in the northwest, achieving its maximum extent between 22,000 and 18,000 years ago. Reaching south to the English Midlands, it was joined for a while to the Scandinavian ice-sheet. Ice over one mile thick covered almost all of Scotland apart from St Kilda, the Orkneys, Buchan and parts of Caithness.

The Shetland Islands had their own separate ice cap.

The treeless tundra promoted by this glacial episode was inhabited by woolly rhinoceros, woolly mammoth, giant elk, wild horse, reindeer, Arctic fox and other suitably adapted animals. Collared lemming and narrow-skulled and northern voles survived underneath the snow. The existence of these bygone inhabitants has been proved by the discovery of fossil remains, such as those of the woolly rhinoceros found in a gravel pit in Bishopbriggs in 1963.

Until 2006 no evidence had been found to prove that humans were present in Scotland before the country's deglaciation. But between 2003 and 2006 the Biggar Archaeology Group of Biggar Museums found a collection of worked flint tools and projectiles which pushed back the previously accepted date for the first known human presence in Scotland by about 3,000 years. The Biggar stones were probably used for killing and processing game; they have been classified by radiocarbon dating and by analysis of their shapes as belonging to the Palaeolithic Era or the Old Stone Age. This suggests that they were used by people who were part of a northwest European culture which depended on following reindeer migrations for its livelihood.

This human presence on the continent's western periphery might well have been sparse and seasonal. Although the exact time and place of the arrival of humans beings in Scotland can never be known, it is extremely significant, for they have exercised a profound influence on Scotland's environment comparable only to that of climate. Over subsequent millennia, human activity would be responsible for a reduction in the numbers and diversity of the country's flora and fauna, alteration and pollution of vegetation and landscapes, and widespread deforestation.

The wasting of the Scottish ice-sheet began around 18,000 years ago but was interrupted around 13,000 years ago by an Arctic cold snap known to palaeoclimatologists as the Loch Lomond Stadial. This phase saw the ice re-extend from Torridon in the northwest as far south as Loch Lomond on the edge of the Highlands. But at a rate contradicting the idea that climate change always occurs gradually, temperatures rose so quickly that within a thousand years Scotland was entirely free of ice apart from individual mountain glaciers in the north and west. The postglacial climate had begun.

Regional Geography

Both the ice and its waning wrought major effects on Scotland's geography, sculpting the regional landscape we know today. Powered by the glaciers' huge mass of ice and then by their vast volumes of meltwater, erosion and deposition shaped the next version of the Scottish environment.

Scotland is a political rather than a bioregional entity. But the country, as it was in its postglacial state, and as it is today, can be broadly divided into four environmental regions: the Highlands and Islands, the Central Lowlands (occupying the Midland Valley), the Southern Uplands and the Eastern Coastal Lowlands. This division is based mainly on major fault lines created at the end of the Caledonian Orogeny, which are visible in satellite images of the country. The elemental differences between these slices of Scotland reflect their different geological origins. The ice and its passing transformed each one of them in different and important ways.

Highlands and Islands

The turbulent Pentland Firth is the Highlands' northern limit and the region's southern edge is the Highland Boundary Fault, which runs diagonally from the Firth of Clyde across Loch Lomond and on to Stonehaven. This fault marks the topographical border between the Highlands and the Central Lowlands. The upland region north of this fault line, bounded by the Eastern Coastal Lowlands, contains a variety of mountainous landforms. The Grampian Mountains occupy the central Highlands south of the Great Glen, and lie southwest to northeast. (The name Grampians may derive indirectly from Mons Graupius, the site of a battle between the Romans and an alliance of native Caledonian tribes at an unknown location in the northeast in 84 ce. Dundonian

Hector Boece, in his *Scotorum Historiæ* (1527), copied the name of the battle site wrongly as Grampius. An early name for this group of mountains was 'The Mounth', from the Gaelic '*monadh*' meaning mountain, which is preserved in Aberdeenshire place-names like Cairn O' Mount. The Grampians, the eroded remains of the Caledonian Mountains, contain the highest summits in Scotland. Ridges and valleys form the steep slopes of the Grampian landscape which contains substantial areas over 800m high.

Drum Alban is the name of the ridge formed by a chain of high mountains running north from Ben Lomond on the east shore of Loch Lomond to Ben Hope in Sutherland. Known by the Romans as part of the Dorsum Britanniae (the Spine of Britain), this watershed was identified by early writers like Adamnan and Bede as a natural boundary between the Picts in the east and the Scots in the west.

North of the Great Glen the upland scenery continues, revealing its gneiss foundations in the 'cnoc and lochan' landscape of low, rounded hills punctured by countless small lochs and peat bogs. Peaks like Beinn Alligan and Sgor Ruadh that stand above this ice-scoured surface in the northwest are the eroded remains of the Torridonian sandstone layer.

During the last ice age, glaciers formed throughout the northern mountains, leaving marked and extensive glacial erosion, especially in the west and northwest, where the relatively warmer and snowier conditions formed glaciers that were thicker and more mobile than those in the east and south. Over 90 per cent of Scotland's rock basins and corries (ice-carved hollows) are in westerly-flowing river systems. In the colder, drier east, where the ice was thinner and less fast flowing, the effects of glacial erosion are less intense.

In the eastern part of the Grampians, glaciers smoothed and rounded the dome-like summits of the granite Cairngorm Mountains, formed during the Caledonian Orogeny. The Cairngorms, extending over 158 square miles, form the largest continuous area of land over 1,000m high in the British Isles and are the site of four of Scotland's five highest mountains.

The schist hills neighbouring the rounded Cairngorms are

craggier, reflecting their fissile nature and the plucking action of glacial ice. In the 300 square miles of the Monadhliath (Grey Hills) which separate Badenoch and Speyside from the Great Glen, weathering and erosion have marked the differences in rock resistance over millions of years. Here the folded metamorphic rocks form striking ridge and valley terrains, generally lower than the Cairngorms, although individual summits like An Sgarsoch reach 1,000m.

Glacial ice streams flowed along existing Highland valleys such as the Great Glen, widening and deepening them into u-shapes and smoothing them by removing rock debris. Glacier ice is relatively soft; its mighty powers of erosion derive from its cargo of rocks and rock debris. Glaciers wore away softer rocks and smoothed off harder ones.

Glacial erosion created more than 500 corries in upland regions of Scotland. It also enlarged existing valleys, creating rock basins that became freshwater lochs when the ice melted. In the west, where successive glaciations had scoured out deep rock basins, over 100 sea-lochs notch the coast. The depth of these basins reflects the erosive power of the ice. For example, the Inner Sound, between Skye and the northern mainland, was carved out by ice that had covered the Applecross mountains and by ice that had been part of Skye's ice cap: it is over 250m deep in parts.

The craggy profiles left by glacial erosion in the northern mountains date from the Loch Lomond Stadial. Peaks like An Teallach and Stac Pollaidh in Wester Ross remained above the ice and were repeatedly shattered by severe frosts, a process which continues today throughout the north.

As the climate warmed, melting ice shaped the Scottish landscape further, depositing glacial till extensively on lower ground. Glacial till – a mix of boulders, sands and gravel – was carried along by ice and meltwater. In the Highlands the glacial deposition of boulder clay was limited to the floors of upland valleys.

The vast volumes of melting ice also caused sea levels to rise, creating 790 islands which became known as the Outer Hebrides chain, the Inner Hebrides and the Orkney and Shetland Islands.

In the far northwest of the mainland and in the Outer Hebrides, the ice eroded the underlying gneiss to form a 'cnoc and lochan' landscape.

The cragginess of the Inner Hebrides is due to their volcanic origins and also to frost repeatedly shattering their summits during the Loch Lomond Stadial. A more subdued relief characterises both Orkney and Shetland; their Old Red Sandstone foundations made the Orkneys more fertile than the Shetland Islands, which are underlain by the same acidic rock as the northwest mainland.

The Central Lowlands and the Eastern Coastal Lowlands

In the Central Lowlands, between the Highland Boundary Fault and the Southern Upland Fault, both glacial deposition and erosion formed the landscape. Most land in the Central Lowlands lies below 175m, but the region does contain volcanic rocks above 600m. Central Lowlands relief was shaped by the differential erosion of its rocks over time. The harder igneous rocks formed hill masses like the Campsie Fells and the Ochils, while the softer sedimentary rocks shaped rolling plains with major river valleys.

When the moving ice met the resistance of the hard volcanic obstacles, streamlined 'crag and tail' features developed (one example being Edinburgh's Royal Mile). Another common feature of glacial erosion, 'roches moutonées', are present in the Highlands and in the Central Lowlands. 'Roches moutonées' were formed by the ice as it smoothed rocks on the glacier's upstream side and plucked rocks on the downstream side. An example of this glacial effect occurred at Grantown-on-Spey.

The Central Lowlands are bordered to the east by the Eastern Coastal Lowlands. The terrain of both regions was formed as glacial deposition produced a generally subdued landscape. The ice-sheets moved down from the mountains, melted and dropped the rocks and rock debris they had been carrying. This covered most of the lower ground with sheets of boulder clay; glacial deposits also formed terraces, ridges and hummocks. The meltwater eroded valleys that were much larger than the rivers that now occupy them. Examples of glacial deposition in the

Central Lowlands include the hummocks or 'drumlins' on which Glasgow is built and the ridges at Carstairs.

Much of the Eastern Coastal Lowlands was formed from till deposited by glaciers and meltwater rivers. Most of the area lies below 200m, though it contains some igneous rocks standing between 300m and 600m, such as the Sidlaws and isolated hills in Buchan. Below these heights, the Eastern Coastal Lowlands undulate gently from the Merse of Berwickshire through the Lothians, Fife, the area east of the Grampians and then further north to the Moray Firth, eastern Sutherland and Caithness.

These coastal lowlands were shaped by the glaciation in another way. As the land was freed of the weight of the melted ice, it gradually sprang upwards and, over time, a new coastline formed at lower levels than the preglacial beaches. Now high above the current sea level and still very gradually rising, these relic 'raised beaches' are covered with loam, silt and clay. Their fertility attracted human settlers from the earliest times.

The Southern Uplands

This region, stretching from Nithsdale to the Eastern Coastal Lowlands, contains a series of hills smoothed and rounded by the action of ice. The Southern Upland ranges include the Lammermuirs, the Moorfoots and the Pentlands. Their scenery is less dramatically craggy than that of the Grampians, with generally lower summits – only a small number are higher than 600m, with very few higher than 800m. In the southwest part of the Southern Uplands, granite masses occur on high ground, including Cairnsmore of Carsphairn, Cairnsmore of Fleet and Crifell. The southern boundary of this region, the Iapetus Suture, also known as the Solway Fault, runs south and parallel to the Southern Uplands Fault.

These diverse postglacial regions together make up the 30,000 square miles of Scotland's land area. The coastline, sharply indented in the west, is 2,300 miles long; nowhere is more than 50 miles from the sea. The mainland measures about 270 miles from the north at Cape Wrath to the south at the Mull of Galloway. At its widest span, from Buchan Ness to Applecross, it measures 154 miles. At its narrowest, between the estuaries of the rivers Clyde and Forth, Scotland is 25 miles wide. In the 13th century the English monk-historian Matthew Paris made the first known geographically representative maps of the British Isles. He shows the Clyde and Forth estuaries almost meeting and marks the land to their north as 'Scotland beyond the Sea'. The bogginess of the Forth crossing at Stirling acted as a deterrent to would-be invaders of northern Scotland, from the Romans to Edward 1.

The volcanic activity on Scotland's western coast that accompanied the opening of the Atlantic Ocean also affected important aspects of mainland geography. The tectonic disturbance created an eastward tilting of the land, which formed a watershed near the west coast draining to the east. The Dee, the Don and the Spey rivers wind east and north into the North Sea, while the Tay (Scotland's longest river at 120 miles) and the Forth flow out from the southern Grampians into the Eastern Coastal Lowlands and then the North Sea. The ceaseless dynamics of tidal erosion and deposition have changed the shape of the eastern coastline since the end of the last ice age: Perth's role as an important sea-port, first for Roman supply ships and later for medieval textile exports, was over by the 1550s after the Tay estuary silted up. The River Tweed rises in the Southern Uplands and meets the North Sea at Berwick. The Clyde also rises in the Southern Uplands but then flows west, as do the rivers Nith and Annan, which empty into the Solway Firth.

Lochs tend to be more numerous and deeper in the north of Scotland than in the south, though soil drainage is a potential problem for human settlement and farming throughout the land. Before the mechanical pumping projects of the 18th and 19th centuries, bogs and marshes were widespread, especially in the Lowlands. The total amount of moisture in the environment is a major feature of the climate and one that has contributed decisively to the environmental history of Scotland's regions.

Soils

Scotland's pattern of regional climatic differences shaped deglactation's living legacy to the Scottish environment: the creation of the country's soils. So often ignored in favour of more picturesque aspects of the environment, soil is supremely important to that environment and its history. Forming a dynamic interface between the Earth's geology and its climate, soil is the foundation for all Scotland's habitats and the ecosystems they support. Soil quality determines the potential of all life within a given area. Before the era of agricultural Improvement the state of each year's local harvest decided outcomes for human life. Harvests depended on the previous twelve months' weather and its effects on soil conditions.

Climate influences soil development profoundly, controlling rates of weathering and decomposition and the accumulation of organic material. Climate is, however, only one of five equally critical factors responsible for the formation of soil. Parent material, such as rock or glacial till, from which the soil evolves influences soil chemistry and texture as well as the soil's ability to absorb and recycle nutrients. The topography of the area where soil evolves determines its drainage and exposure. The vegetation and organisms growing in the soil nourish and mix it and help its accumulation of organic matter. Time is the last key factor necessary for the complex processes of soil formation to take place.

In fact, as deglaciated environments in Alaska and Iceland have shown, vegetation can develop on land only a few centuries after it has been scoured clean by ice and meltwater. At the end of the last ice age, glacial deposits were first colonised by microorganisms and plants that converted these deposits into living and productive soil. Marked variations in soil-forming factors led to the development of different soils in different places, and sometimes to no soil at all.

The four main types of soil that formed after the ice melted were peats, podsols, gleys and brown forest earths. Modified by time, climate change and increasingly powerful human activity mixed together to form Scotland's varied soils.

Peat is produced when dead plant material accumulates faster than soil-forming processes can break it up. Basin peat builds up in damp lowland hollows; blanket peat forms in the cool wet conditions of the Scottish uplands. Blanket peat is more widespread, being formed chiefly from sphagnum mosses. They can dominate peatlands thanks to their ability to absorb nutrients directly from rainwater.

Podsols occur at all levels throughout Scotland, forming where water drains freely through the soil and leaches away organic matter and nutrients. Despite their infertility, podsols support acid-tolerating vegetation such as heather and coniferous woodland.

Gley soils, found all over Scotland, are produced by permanent or intermittent waterlogging. Poor drainage may result from its high content of impermeable clay or its position at the foot of a slope or in a hollow. Waterlogging causes an absence of oxygen in gley soils, chemically altering the iron they contain, which limits their fertility and causes their characteristic bluish-grey appearance.

By contrast, the iron content of brown forest earth gives fertility and a rich colour to soils originally formed under the country's first deciduous woodlands, especially in warm, dry and sheltered areas. Forest soils are well drained, non-acidic and rich in nutrients.

Of Scotland's postglacial soils, those forming in the northwest and the Outer Hebrides tended to be more acidic because of the cool wet upland climate and the acidity of much of the underlying parent material. Harsh climatic conditions further disadvantaged soil formation: Atlantic gales and salt spray limited biological activity, including tree growth and the consequent production of leaf humus and its valuable nutrients. With no vegetation to protect the young soil from exposure to heavy rainfall, podsolisation leached minerals and made it even more acidic and infertile. However, original tree cover was more widely established in other upland areas in the warm conditions that prevailed until after the arrival of the human population. Trees grew on brown forest soils that developed where glacial till had been deposited in sheltered upland valleys in the southwest and in the Highlands.

Fertile soils formed most extensively in the Central Lowlands and the Eastern Coastal Lowlands. These lowland areas, underlain by sedimentary rock, were relatively warm and sheltered. Topography also contributed to the development of brown forest soils, which occurred where glacial till was deposited on sheltered low ground that was also fairly flat. Relative warmth and non-acidic conditions meant that vegetation grew, organic matter was effectively broken down and earthworms flourished. The resulting plant cover protected the young soil from podsolisation and enriched it with leaf humus.

Farming in the southern end of the Eastern Coastal Lowlands benefited both from soil fertility and the innovations of Romans, Angles and Cistercians. The region's high levels of agricultural productivity led to its early involvement in Scotland's cash economy and to the adoption there of modern farming methods as early as the 17th century.

Soil developed differently throughout Scotland's island groups. A wide variety of soil types formed on the Hebrides. Tree cover was slow to develop on all of Scotland's islands because of their exposure to strong winds and salt spray. Cool climate, exposure to the Atlantic and thin acidic soil prohibited tree growth altogether on Lewis and Harris. Peat formed extensively throughout the Outer Hebrides.

A unique type of soil cover evolved on the western coasts of the Outer Hebrides and isolated parts of the mainland, the northern islands and the west coast of Ireland. In these coastal areas, glaciers and their meltwaters washed sand and gravels into the sea. Tidal currents then spread the sediments along the coasts where they mixed with vast quantities of crushed shells of molluscs and other marine creatures. This mixture was subsequently driven ashore by the powerful action of Atlantic winds and waves. The result was the formation of beaches and dunes of white shelly sand which were then dispersed inland by the wind, creating the essential foundations of the machair.

In Gaelic, machair means a low fertile plain; the human

contribution to this unique landscape would not be made until the era of the Neolithic farmers. They grew crops of barley on the rich machair soils which they fertilised with kelp (laminaria), a species of seaweed also known as tangle. As well as enriching the machair's sandy soil, kelp kept it moist, consolidated and protected from erosion by the wind. Dung from cattle also enhanced the machair's soil structure and fertility. Today's enchanting machair landscapes have developed from human use of the lime-rich postglacial environment. The country's more acidic environments experienced a less productive relationship with primitive agriculture.

The Inner Hebrides contain areas where very hard volcanic rocks promote thin soils. But throughout the islands these are mixed with more fertile patches of earth formed on limestone and sandstone. Productive soil often underlay the development of political power. For example, significant amounts of limestone enrich the islands of Lismore and Islay: the former became the seat of a bishopric and the latter the power base of the Lordship of the Isles.

Deglaciation left a fertile glacial till covering the Orkneys but Shetland's more acidic rocks and exposed topography meant that only the coastal margin retained enough mineral content to be fertile.

So, by approximately 11,000 years ago, all of Scotland had been transformed by climate change from an Arctic wasteland to a rich and varied environment with habitats for the warmth-loving plants and animals that were the country's first colonists.

Postglacial Colonists

As well as enabling tree growth in much of Scotland, the warming of the climate caused the extinction of animals that had lived on the tundra. The wild horse, Arctic fox, collared lemming and northern and narrow-skulled voles all disappeared in the early postglacial period as the warming climate destroyed their Arctic habitats.

According to fossil evidence, the wild horse failed to adapt to the woodlands that replaced Scotland's open plains, although it continued to flourish in the forests of the European mainland. Evidence is scarce, but a horse bone found in the Pentland Hills has been radiocarbon-dated to approximately 10,000 years before the present (bp) and it shows that the species was about one third the size of a modern horse. Reindeer survived in Scotland until the tundra had been completely replaced by woodlands; the most recent original reindeer remains found in Scotland have been radiocarbon-dated at 8300 bp.

Some species did adapt to postglacial conditions in the northern uplands. The Arctic hare (also called the blue or mountain hare) evolved as a separate sub-species (lepus timidus scoticus), with its thick white winter coat indicating Arctic heritage. Another living relic of the ice age is the ptarmigan (lagopus mutus). Related to the grouse, it lives on Highland mountain summits, retaining an all-white winter plumage. (At the time of writing, Scottish Natural Heritage has expressed concern that climate change is threatening these habitats and the species they support.)

As the climate continued to warm, the postglacial environment assembled. Knowledge of this early vegetation and the climate that supported it is based on the analysis of fossilised spores and pollen. Fossilised pollen grains have a wide range of shapes, sizes and surface markings characteristic of each individual species (many are spherical, while those of pines are winged). Pollen analysis shows that juniper, dwarf willow and rowan, remnants of the vanishing tundra, were among the first species to respond to Scotland's warming climate and growing soil cover. Eleven thousand years ago, these shrubs began to dominate a land also covered with grasses, sedges and mosses. Within another 1,000 years, trees were growing all over Scotland from seeds brought on the wind and by birds.

Species arrived in a sequence that depended on how distant their origins were. Birch from the south of Britain was the first to arrive and in the next millennium it combined with hazel to cover most of Scotland, forcing the shrubs of the former tundra to colonise the higher ground.

The warm climate continued to encourage tree cover capable

of nourishing the developing soils. Elm and oak, responding to rising temperatures, appeared in Scotland 8,000–9,000 years ago and spread slowly northwards. At about the same time, Scots pine (pinus sylvestris) arrived, possibly from seed originating in Ireland. It became established in sheltered parts of the northwest, where it flourished in the colder conditions. Woodland remained scarce on all the islands and throughout exposed parts of the northwest.

For seven millennia after the retreat of the glaciers, the warming climate continued to encourage tree growth throughout the Scottish mainland. At the climax of this growth, around 5,000 years ago, tree lines were over one third higher than today's upper limits. This rich woodland environment attracted animals with its shelter and food resources. New species of animals and birds migrated to Scotland as woodland formed from a patchwork of different trees.

The remains of animals preserved in peatbog and clay provide a record of the species that lived in Scotland after the ice disappeared. Some like the Arctic hare and the Arctic lemming must have come from the European mainland while cold conditions still prevailed. Many species – and their human predators – travelled across lands that joined the south and east of Britain to northern France, the Low Countries, north Germany and Denmark. This migration ended when the rising water levels produced by melting glaciers submerged all land connections to Europe, leaving Scotland and the rest of Britain with less mammal species than the continental mainland. Ireland has even less native mammal species; its land link to Britain was submerged earlier than the one between Britain and the continent.

Scotland's first woodland-dwelling animals included elk, a large species of deer whose remains have been found all over northern Scotland. Red deer roamed everywhere; roe deer were scarcer. Aurochs were also present, their remains having been discovered at over 40 sites. These primitive oxen had evolved in India two million years earlier and then migrated to Europe via the Middle East and Asia, arriving 250,000 years ago. Aurochs were big: Julius Caesar compared the aurochs he saw on campaign in the German forests to elephants. Their withers were 1.75m high compared to the 1.4m of modern cows. Their huge, flat-fronted heads, about one third bigger than those of modern cows, carried immense horns. Aurochs had none of their domesticated descendants' placidity: the vicious aggression of the modern African buffalo gives a better idea of their temperament. Caesar warned: 'Great is their strength and great their speed; they spare nor man nor wild beast on whom they cast their eyes.'

The wild boar remains found in Scotland indicate a once significant population. Badgers and squirrels also inhabited the ancient woodlands, with otters and beavers living on rivers. The chief animal predators in the woodland environment were lynx, brown bear and wolf; there were also the lesser carnivores – stoat, weasel, wildcat and fox, all of which could become the quarry of the hunter-gatherers, who had successfully adapted to warmer conditions.

2

Humans Arrive in Scotland

Mesolithic Scotland

THE FIRST NOMADIC hunter-gatherers were few in number and their lifestyle made extensive but largely sustainable demands on the environment. There is a relative scarcity of archaeological evidence from the Mesolithic (Middle Stone Age) epoch, which lasted in northern Europe from c.9000 bp to c.6000 bp. Scotland and Ireland were among the last lands in Europe to be colonised by humans.

Some of Scotland's first Mesolithic colonists may have arrived across the ice-sheet extending from southern Norway to the Orkneys and the fertile plains of the northeast mainland. Mesolithic colonisation from the continent continued to occur across the continental land links to south and east Britain. The marshy environment of these links held valuable food resources for the hunter-gatherers. Their submersion, as glacial meltwater forced up sea levels, may have prompted an influx of hunter-gatherers looking for new territory. Mesolithic settlers also arrived by sea from the southwest.

Warm summers and cold winters were still promoting woodland growth throughout Scotland. Colonists would have looked inland at a wilderness of virgin woodland, possibly settling on one of the raised beaches formed by the passing of the ice. In fact, many Mesolithic sites identified in Scotland are in the south and west, although this may be because more intensive agriculture in the east has obliterated remnants there.

The MacArthur Cave near Oban was excavated in 1895–96 and the shell-middens on the southern Hebridean island of Oronsay were investigated three years later. Shell-middens are the highly informative remains of the hunter-gatherers' kitchen refuse piles, enduring because the calcium carbonate content of the shells counteracts the soil's usual corrosiveness. Evidence of Mesolithic activity has subsequently been detected in the Central Lowlands, on the east coast and as far north as the shores of the Pentland Firth. The National Museums of Scotland have Mesolithic exhibits from all over Scotland including Lussa Bay (Jura), Doonfoot (Ayrshire), Rink Farm (Selkirkshire), Banchory (Aberdeenshire) and various locations in Orkney. Scotland's earliest Mesolithic settlement was discovered during excavations of a Roman site at Cramond (near Edinburgh), where pits and stakeholes indicate a hunter-gatherer encampment. Mesolithic finds included burnt hazelnut shells, elk bones, fish bones and shellfish, all radiocarbon-dated to around 9000 bp. Since 1999 archaeologists from the 'Scotland's First Settlers' project of Edinburgh University have been unearthing signs of an extended Mesolithic community in the Inner Hebrides. These sites have revealed many important aspects of Mesolithic life in Scotland. Hunter-gatherers lived on coasts, on islands and inland. They were nomadic, staying in skin shelters or caves and moving on when local food resources were used up. They used river valleys, lochs and indented seacoasts to penetrate wooded hinterlands. Some of their routes are visible in modern settlement patterns. Remains of Mesolithic dugout canoes have been found in Scandinavia and Ireland and Scotland's Mesolithic settlers might well have used similar craft for sea journeys and inland navigation.

Woods were not an obstacle to the hunter-gatherers; indeed, they used the whole postglacial environment to meet their needs. Woodlands provided cover for shelter and hunting. As the contents of inland and coastal middens show, the environment offered a wide variety of foodstuffs to Mesolithic people, who moved through the landscape following migrations of the animals and fish they hunted and seasons of the plants they harvested.

This ceaseless mobility is one reason for the scarcity of Mesolithic remains. The acidic nature of the Scottish environment is another. The acidity of much of Scotland's soil has destroyed Mesolithic artefacts made of organic materials like bone, antler and horn. The great age of Mesolithic remains also makes for their rarity and some Mesolithic sites were occupied through the Neolithic and Bronze Ages, confusing the dates of archaeological finds. However, shell-middens and stones have been found which do reveal information on Mesolithic diets and livelihoods.

West coast shell-middens contain a huge variety of marine species including periwinkles, whelks, mussels, scallops, cockles, razor shells, oysters and limpets. Fish bones belonging to saithe, spiny dogfish, skate, haddock, angelfish, conger eel, grey mullet and black sea-bream have also been discovered in the middens. Near the east coast they contain remains of cod, salmon and sea-trout. Mesolithic people may have used fish traps made of pliable wood such as willow.

Seabirds well represented in Mesolithic middens include gannets, shags, geese, cormorants, gulls, razorbills, guillemots, terns and ducks. On Oronsay and on the island of Risga at the mouth of Loch Sunart, middens have been discovered containing the bones of the great auk. This flightless bird, also known as the garefowl, was last seen in Scotland on the St Kilda archipelago in the 1820s and became globally extinct shortly afterwards.

Scotland's Mesolithic middens have also been found to contain the bones of slaughtered mammals, including elk, red deer, auroch, roe deer and wild pig, while coastal middens reveal bones from whales, dolphins, and grey and common seals.

Inevitably, little evidence of non-meat consumption has survived, but studies of modern hunter-gatherers suggests that the Mesolithic diet is likely to have been composed of perhaps as much as 80 per cent vegetable matter. Quantities of hazel nutshells have been found on many Mesolithic sites and it is very probable that other nuts, wild fruits, berries, seeds, fungi, roots, bulbs, grasses and weeds like fat-hen (chenopodium album) and corn spurry (spergularia arvensis) dominated Mesolithic diets.

Archaeological evidence reveals that stone was a major component in Mesolithic life. Fire-blackened hearthstones from this era indicate the presence of campfires where carcasses of hunted animals were butchered and roasted. Fires did make permanent Mesolithic marks on the environment: they left charcoal layers in peat though some of these deposits may result from lightning. Mesolithic groups used fire to eradicate patches of vegetation for new campsites. Hunters may have used fire-clearance to help sight prey in woodlands and to encourage plants likely to attract particular animals.

Flint, chert, agate, quartz and amethyst were modified by prehistoric humans intent on increasing their power to manipulate and exploit the environment. Mesolithic innovations significantly enhanced these powers. Flint is relatively rare in Scotland, with Morven in the northwest an important source. Quartz, although harder to work, was commonly used. Stoneworkers used harder hammerstones to make chosen stones shatter, then worked the flakes to make the Mesolithic *tour de force*: the microlith. These delicate, razor-sharp blades were used for cutting, tool-making and for the first projectile weapons.

This technological revolution was the hunters' response to changing environmental conditions. Palaeolithic (Old Stone Age) people had been able to cull the herds of reindeer roaming the tundra. The dense forest cover of Mesolithic times contained evasive prey, notably elk, red deer and aurochs. Brute force and human numbers were no longer enough. Hunter-gatherers met the new challenges with microlithic weapons. They made harpoons, spears and arrows by fitting the sharpened flint fragments onto wooden or bone hafts. This technical advance restored their advantage over their animal prey.

Stones identified at Sand on the Applecross peninsula originated across the Inner Sound and further afield. Stone for making Mesolithic tools came from the island of Rum (18 miles to the south) and Staffin on Skye (six miles to the west).

The hunter-gatherers used microliths as scrapers and gougers to make artefacts from bone, antler and horn, including barbed points, awls and pins. Barbed points improve the deadly efficiency of arrowheads and fish hooks, making them harder for prey to dislodge. Grooved and furrowed pebbles have also been found, which were used for grinding to increase the sharpness of microliths and hence their lethal effectiveness. Microliths were also central to food processing, being used to extract flesh from shellfish and to gut and skin animals. Skins were used to make clothes and tents. Mesolithic hunter-gatherers practised leather-tanning and the preservation of animal flesh by smoking.

They also made larger, stronger and more durable flint tools, axes for cutting timber and hammers for knocking limpets off rocks. On some Mesolithic sites shells have been found with signs of wear that suggest their use as scoops or ladles. Jewellery made from decorated shell has also been discovered. Self-adornment has also been suggested by the widespread presence of ochre on Mesolithic sites. Archaeologists at Applecross found ochre and a species of dog-whelk from which purple dye can be made. We might therefore surmise that the hunter-gatherers had time and energy for more than basic survival.

It is tempting to romanticise Mesolithic freedom. But to do so is to forget the constant and extreme uncertainty which dominated nomadic life. Climatic and other disasters could fatally remove expected food resources. As well as threats of famine and storm, the inhabitants of flimsy, transient campsites faced constant danger from a variety of predators, including lynx, bear, auroch and wolf. Mesolithic people feasted on bear and auroch when they got the chance, but because of these animals' ferocity and cunning they would have had to seize that chance very circumspectly. The high mobility of Mesolithic communities made vulnerable anyone immobilised by old age, injury or illness; these unfortunates would face falling behind and losing the protection of the group.

The significance of the Mesolithic era in Scotland is immense, witnessing as it does the use of technology to increase human control over the environment – the beginning of a complex and enthralling story. The hunter-gatherers utilised the environment in their quest for food and shelter and other resources while that same environment also limited many aspects of their existence. Food resources were only available at certain times and under certain conditions, and shelter was only viable where landscape and vegetation allowed. Human survival depended on a deep working understanding of all aspects of the environment. It is hard to imagine that such an understanding did not breed a powerful respect for the environment, even if we cannot know what forms such respect took. But there is one thing that we can be certain about: the hunter-gatherers were the last humans to have such a limited impact on Scotland's environment.

3

The Beginnings of Farming

AROUND 6,000 YEARS ago throughout Scotland's lowlands, uplands and islands, human activity started to undergo a radical transformation that would have immense repercussions for relationships between the land's human inhabitants and its non-human environment. New ways of making a living had profound, multiple and permanent effects on the environment and fostered entirely new attitudes to it. The beginning of agriculture in Scotland started a process in which human impacts on the environment became ever more powerful.

The phase of human evolution that inspired this shift saw nomadic lifestyles replaced by a settled farming existence which depended on the adoption (forced or voluntary) of a package of innovations pioneered in the Fertile Crescent of the Middle East around 10–11,000 years ago.

The Fertile Crescent extends from the eastern Mediterranean coast through the valley of the Tigris and Euphrates to the Persian Gulf. It was here that humans first exploited local plant and animal species by farming, a development that may have been a response to the hunter-gatherers' exhaustion of game and other food resources. Water shortages resulting from climate change could also have undermined the viability of their livelihoods, forcing them to settle by rivers.

Whatever prompted this revolutionary transformation, these were the first humans to live in permanently settled communities. Their increasing sophistication was made possible by the extra time and energy guaranteed by food surpluses. The new types of human activity are classified as Neolithic or belonging to the New Stone Age. They had profound consequences for human and animal life all over the globe, starting with the founding of the first major civilisations in Assyria, Sumeria and Babylon.

Domestication of wild species by breeding or cultivation was central to the pastoral and arable elements of Neolithic life. Local plants such as barley and emmer wheat became the first farmed cereal crops. Bred for size and yield were oxen, sheep, goats and pigs, which were also selected for docility. The animals' manure fertilised the crops. For the first time in their history humans had the chance to accumulate food and challenge their permanent vulnerability to famine.

Knowledge of the new farming methods and the stock and seed they required spread west and north from the Fertile Crescent, reaching Egypt in a millennium and central Europe in another. Immigrants from Europe and from southern Britain were the first to undertake Neolithic activities in Scotland but their example was soon followed by at least some native hunter-gatherers.

Other developments, including milking, the wheel and metalwork evolved as a result of the time, energy and specialised effort now available to the human population thanks to greater and more reliable food yields offered by farming. Food surpluses also enabled the development of organised religion with a powerful priesthood and the creation of the symbolic stone monuments of which Scotland has an impressive heritage. These structures originally acted as territorial markers as well as foci for social organisation.

Hunter-gathering tribes changed into fully-fledged settled farming communities at different rates. Some adopted elements of the Neolithic package, such as the cultivation of crop plants, while continuing to be partly nomadic and using mobile camps from which to harvest wild food. Neolithic societies may have evolved earliest in Scotland's western and northern islands, where more evidence of primitive field systems has been found than on the mainland (where it may simply have been obliterated by greater agricultural activity on the mainland). But the islands' position on important sea routes certainly made them more accessible to the arrival of new ideas.

Superior harvests were ultimately responsible for this diffusion of Neolithic farming methods. In any struggle over land or resources, Neolithic tribes would have had many advantages over Mesolithic opponents: they were better fed, being in receipt of far more calories per acre, and were better equipped with domesticated animals which provided transport, ropes and fibres. They displaced or simply out-bred Mesolithic tribes; intervals between births were shorter for the Neolithic people, thanks to their diet. Later advances in bronze, and then iron technology were even more decisive. During the Bronze and Iron Ages the Neolithic revolution took hold throughout Scotland. No archaeological evidence of mass invasion has been found: Neolithic transformation would not seem to have been the result of brute force but rather of the spread of ideas.

By 5000 bp, most of Scotland's human inhabitants had become at least part-time farmers. Neolithic middens show that these first farmers supplemented their agricultural diet with wild resources, including seabirds, fish, shellfish, deer and whales. The mixed (arable and pastoral) subsistence agriculture established in prehistoric Scotland endured until the 18th century. Well before then, however, this primitive agriculture, expanding in scale as populations increased, began to make permanent marks on the Scottish environment.

Although the first farmers left far more of an impression on the Scottish environment than did the hunter-gatherers, archaeological evidence of the early Neolithic period in Scotland is still too limited for more than general conclusions to be made about the period's environmental history. However, evidence from individual sites such as Eilean Domnhuill (North Uist), Knap of Howar and Skara Brae (Orkney), Balbridie (Aberdeenshire) and Boghead (Moray) provides an outline of the relationship between early Neolithic farmers and their environment.

Fossilised cereal pollen and the presence of querns (grinding stones) show that cereal cultivation was taking place on all these sites. Neolithic choice of cereal species varied. At different times, barley was favoured at Boghead and Skara Brae, and bere and emmer wheat at Balbridie. Bere (hordeum sativum) is an ancient form of barley that tolerates northern Scotland's cool climate and short growing season. Cereal cultivation was only part of the Neolithic revolution. Findings on all of these sites of the bones of domesticated animals with butchery marks are evidence of the first communities in Scotland based on the rearing and slaughter of animals for food. One of the most significant modifications of the Scottish environment made throughout prehistory was the introduction of these domesticated animal species: goats, cows, pigs and sheep.

Domesticated Species

Sheep

There is no evidence for the presence of sheep in Scotland between the end of the last ice age and the Neolithic period. Early Neolithic incomers brought their own sheep to Scotland as an important element of their agriculture. The nature of these Stone Age animals differed greatly from that of their modern descendants, which are the product of selective breeding of primitive sheep for various human requirements. Occurring over millennia, this process has changed the original species almost beyond recognition. However, owing to the geographical remoteness of their original locations in Scotland, two distinct and pure examples of the Neolithics' primitive sheep have survived.

Soay, a rocky island in the St Kilda archipelago, has given its name to one of these ancient breeds, probably brought there by St Kilda's first Neolithic settlers around 4,000 years ago. Around 3,000 years later, Norse invaders named the archipelago 'Saudaey', Island of Sheep. St Kilda lies in the North Atlantic, 40 miles west of the Outer Hebrides. This extreme isolation ensured the survival of the Neolithic breed, unaltered, into modern times. These animals were of key importance to human existence on the islands, providing fat, meat, milk and fibres. When the human population was evacuated from St Kilda in 1930, the thousands of Soay sheep left in possession survived, reverting to their original wild nature.

Soay sheep are descended from the wild Mouflon that originated in Mediterranean regions and are still found in Corsica and Sardinia. The breed was present throughout southern and central Europe in Neolithic times and its Soay descendants retain Mouflon characteristics. With their slender limbs, agility and shyness, they are far more reminiscent of goats than of modern breeds of sheep. Males and females have thick, goat-like horns that curve backwards and then down around their heads. Their wool, which they shed, is usually dark brown, tan or less commonly, black.

Scotland's other extant primitive breed of sheep, the Peat, or Turbary, is also related to the Mouflon, though it had a more northerly European distribution in Neolithic times. Bones belonging to this species have been found in Neolithic middens all over northern Scotland. Again, geographical isolation ensured that relatively unaltered descendants of these primitive sheep survive on the Shetland Islands. They are of the same small size as Soay sheep and have similarly shaped horns but their wool has a wider range of colours including white, moorit (reddish brown), silvery grey, fawn, dark brown and black. Shetland sheep have to be sheared. medieval Scotland's huge flocks of dun-coloured sheep were descended from Neolithic animals, as were those used in the creation of modern sheep breeds by the agricultural Improvers of the 18th century.

Cows

The auroch (bos taurus primigenius) was present throughout Scotland until the Iron Age. Numbers dwindled under pressure from Neolithic hunters and they gravitated northwards, seeking shelter from the increasingly numerous human populations of the fertile Lowlands. The bones of butchered cattle found in Neolithic middens from Orkney to Dumfriesshire belong to an entirely different species of cattle, the Celtic shorthorn (bos taurus longifrons). Like Mouflon sheep, Celtic shorthorns were brought as domesticates to Scotland by Neolithic immigrants. In both Highland and Lowland middens their bones predominate; their meat continued to be a major Scottish food resource well into the Middle Ages.

The aurochs' vicious temperament made them unsuitable for domestication. However, some interbreeding between aurochs and Celtic shorthorns must have taken place in Scotland and on the continent, with the auroch legacy clearly visible in large-boned modern breeds like the Aberdeen Angus.

In contrast, the skull of the Celtic shorthorn was narrow, more like that of a deer than of a modern cow. It had a bony ridge carrying two short, tapering horns about nine inches long, which curved gently forward and downwards. Skeletal remains show that the Celtic shorthorn was long-bodied but light and nimble: well adapted for avoiding woodland predators. The semi-wild nature of these domesticates is indicated in Celtic shorthorn remains by their young age at slaughter, confirmed by the presence of milk teeth and immature bones. This slaughtering of young beasts suggests the breed still retained their wild characteristics, with older beasts too strong and wily to catch. Bone remains also demonstrate the beasts' high mobility: a sign of their enduring wildness. Neolithic farmers did not enclose their cattle but allowed them to range.

White cattle, like those kept today at Chillingham in Northumbria, appear throughout Scottish folklore and literature. White cattle dwelling in the mythical Caledonian forest were supposed to produce especially delectable meat. However, it seems most likely that any herds of wild white cattle present in the historic Scottish countryside were descendants of aurochs that had bred with domesticated cows in Neolithic times.

Horses

Shetland and Highland ponies are considered natives of Scotland but as the native Scottish horse did not survive the postglacial habitat change from open plains to woodland, it can be assumed that these breeds are descended from animals brought by immigrants. By the 19th century many of the Hebridean islands, including Rum, Barra and Skye, had given their names to individual breeds of pony; but all these types originated from Neolithic imports.

Horse bones have been found on various Neolithic sites, including Ardrossan and at Loch Stennis (Orkney). Like Neolithic sheep, these horses adapted well to the harsh conditions of both mainland and islands and certainly these creatures have been in Scotland for a very, very long time. Tacitus noted small, hardy horses yoked to the chariots of the native tribes in his account of their battle against Roman invasion forces at Mons Graupius.

Pigs

The contents of Neolithic middens show that pigs were an important element in Scotland's Neolithic agriculture. Wild boar was present in the postglacial Scottish environment and became prey for the hunter-gatherers. Like auroch, boar would have been a challenging quarry. Both male and female stood over a metre high at the shoulder and weighed around 200 and 130 kilograms respectively. Their bristly coats were red, brown or black and covered a powerful body, with a big head, erect ears and shoulders tapering to smaller hindquarters.

The relative smallness of butchered pig bones at Neolithic Skara Brae suggests that wild boars were at least partly domesticated by the early farmers. However, the loss of forest habitat throughout Scotland and the corruption of the species' indigenous gene pool by escaped domesticates meant that Scotland's original wild boar was probably extinct before the 17th century. Escapees and hybrid crosses between them and remaining wild stock formed semi-wild herds all over Scotland. By the Middle Ages, their scavenging instincts were taking care of urban waste disposal, although by the 15th century these herds were perceived as a worthless nuisance. However, like primitive sheep, these pigs were ancestors to modern breeds.

Goats

Goats are generally thought to have been brought to Scotland by Neolithic settlers for meat, milk and hides. Upland dwellers benefited from their hardiness and ability to survive on meagre winter rations, provided they had adequate shelter. Goats (especially billies) have a tendency to stray, which caused the establishment of feral flocks of escapees throughout the land.

Common Vole

The common vole, microtus arvalis, was carried to the Orkney Islands in the boats of Neolithic settlers. Having no natural predators there, the vole developed a larger body size than its modern descendants. Subsequent deterioration in the voles' environment reduced their size to its modern proportions.

Cats and Dogs

Given their relatively small numbers, cats and dogs probably created slight impacts on the prehistoric Scottish environment. However, both were important elements of the Neolithic regime. Their presence in primitive farming settlements, guarding grain stores against vermin and protecting livestock from predators, was yet another aspect, like selective animal breeding and monument building, of humans' increasing manipulation of their environment. Cats and dogs were among the animals deified by the ancient Egyptians. The earliest record of domesticated cats dates from Egypt *c.*3500 bp. At the Howe on Orkney evidence has been found that cats were among the animals kept by the group of families settled there in the Bronze Age; they may also have kept cats as pets.

There is evidence from the Mesolithic era in England that

hunter-gatherers used dogs for hunting and so this may well have been the case in Scotland. Certainly, dog bones have been found on Neolithic sites throughout Scotland though dogs' physiological similarity to the wolves that menaced prehistoric settlements makes definite identification difficult.

The environmental effects of the Scotland's Neolithic civilisation were not confined to the import of individual species. The introduction of farming also entailed momentous consequences for native species and their habitats.

Persecution, Hybridisation and Extinction: Prehistoric Agriculture's Impact on Scotland's Animals

The first farming communities' efficient and purposeful attitude to their environment had significant consequences for the animals and vegetation within it. Expanding Neolithic populations supplemented their diet by hunting game and fish and they systematically attacked the flora and fauna that threatened their crops and flocks. James Ritchie, Assistant Keeper in the Natural History Department of the Royal Scottish Museum, in his masterpiece, *The Influence of Man on Animal Life in Scotland* (1920), recognised the implications of the Neolithic agenda for Scotland's fauna: '[their] casual slaughter of prowling animals developed into enmity and a blood feud against the larger beasts and birds of prey.' This enmity increased as human populations expanded.

Birds of prey threatening livestock included buzzards, red kites, golden eagles and sea eagles (known as 'ernes' to medieval Scots). Some Neolithic communities treated the larger birds of prey with totemic respect, using eagle feathers in human burial practices. But raptors menaced pastoral subsistence: eagles can take a single lamb in their claws and, like buzzards, can bring down adult beasts after pecking out their eyes. Neolithic weaponry, limited to spears and bows and arrows tipped with microliths, had a limited effect on birds. Large beasts of prey were easier to kill and threatened the human population and their flocks more directly. The growing efficacy of direct human action against both predators and prey is indicated by the roll-call of extinctions occurring in Scotland since the start of human colonisation and hunting by humans is heavily implicated in the demise of some species.

Human activity also caused extinctions indirectly. Hybridisation with members of domesticated animals corrupted the gene pools of certain native species, such as auroch and wild boar. Habitat loss, when clearings were made for crops and herds, also undermined the viability of some indigenous species. Scotland's forest-dwelling creatures were fatally vulnerable to reductions in tree cover.

Lynx remains, preserved in Craig nan Uamh, a limestone cave near Inchnadamph in Sutherland, have been radiocarbon-dated to around 2000 bp, well after the hunter-gatherers' era. This suggests the species was not hunted to extinction for food but rather to protect Neolithic settlements and their flocks.

Auroch are thought to have survived in Scotland till the Iron Age, around 2,500 years ago. Their extinction was the product of coinciding factors. Interbreeding with imported Celtic shorthorn cattle reduced their numbers. The threat they posed to humans intensified their persecution; they were also hunted for their meat and hide. But probably the most significant factor in the aurochs' decline was habitat loss caused by the reduction in Scotland's woodland cover from c.6000 bp.

4

The First Permanent Modifications to Postglacial Vegetation

WHEN THE NEOLITHIC settlers arrived woodland covered over 50 per cent of Scotland's land surface. The country had never been entirely enveloped by forest: fewer trees grew on coasts, flood plains, montane plateaux and islands. In parts of northwest Scotland conditions had restricted soil-forming processes from the start of the postglacial era. But in other parts of the country, including some sheltered upland areas, brown forest soils developed and supported woodland environments.

By the start of the 18th century woodland cover had shrunk to approximately one twentieth of Scotland's land surface. It began a very slow recovery with the (sometimes non-native) plantations of the 18th century agricultural Improvers. Today, virtually treeless moorlands and peatlands cover nearly one third of Scotland's land area and underlie some of the country's most iconic landscapes and globally important habitats. What caused these changes and how they affected human and non-human life are questions central to Scotland's environmental history.

That substantial deforestation had occurred throughout Scotland by the early modern period is confirmed by reports made by visitors to the country. Elizabethan traveller Fynes Moryson said of Fife, 'Trees are so scarce that I remember not to have seen one wood.' In 1617 Sir Anthony Weldon claimed nastily, 'Judas could not have found a tree in all Scotland on which to hang himself.' Certainly, extensive imports of Baltic and Scandinavian timber were a fact of Scottish economic life by late medieval times. Blame for the decline of Scotland's postglacial forests and the spread of relatively infertile peat and moorland environments has been directed at a variety of culprits, often outsiders. These include Romans, Vikings and the army of Oliver Cromwell. Eighteenth century ironmasters have been accused of consuming Scottish woodlands in their charcoal smelters. The vast numbers of sheep brought in during the Highland Clearances have also been charged with destroying habitats and landscapes, as well as human communities. However, to understand what did happen to Scotland's original tree cover, the chronology of forest decline must first be established.

In his article on Scottish woodland history in *Scotland Since Prehistory* (1993), TC Smout warns that blaming invaders for their destruction of Scotland's forest cover by fire or sword is vastly to overestimate their potential impact on the environment. Hand-felled woodland regenerates in time, pine flourishes after fire and important deciduous species like birch and oak are hard to eliminate by burning.

The Romans arrived in Scotland sometime after 79 ce. Agricola sent a fleet to survey the coasts of the little-known land north of the territory secured by the invaders since 43 ce. Agricola, general and provincial governor of Britain 78–89 ce, was able to subdue much of southern Scotland but found the northern tribes more resistant. Tacitus reports that as the Romans advanced, the northern tribes they called the Caledonii 'turned to armed resistance on a large scale'. The Caledonii conducted locally devastating raids on Roman positions and threatened to wipe out isolated Roman forces.

The fighting culminated in 84 ce at the battle of Mons Graupius. The Roman historians who recorded the slow progress of Agricola's campaign emphasised the difficulties that the great forest of Caledon presented to the imperial troops. These reports beguiled European scholars for centuries, encouraging later assumptions that vast numbers of Scottish trees had suffered heavy damage at the hands of the Romans.

These tales of forests on the empire's distant frontier are better understood as a metaphorical description of the many practical difficulties that the Romans encountered fighting a guerrilla war in cold, mountainous and boggy conditions. Smout (1993) elegantly confirms the mythical nature of Caledon. He points out that the Romans' look-out posts on the Gask ridge, west of Perth, could only have commanded strategic views in a generally treeless landscape. As he observes, modern conifer plantations now obscure views of Glenalmond and Strathearn from the ridge where the Romans had their vantage points.

So it was not dark forests but the strength of the native tribes and their territory's challenging terrain which prevented the Romans achieving effective control over northern Scotland. Emperor Hadrian's visit to Britain in 122 ce convinced him that these natives could never be assimilated into the Roman empire. He decided to counter their threat by constructing a permanent and substantial barrier against their incursions. Hadrian's Wall was a stone and timber structure stretching 73 miles from Wallsend on the east coast to Bowness on the west; it was built over the six years following Hadrian's visit. Studded with forts, fortlets and towers, the wall was the first piece of human engineering to dominate Scotland's landscape on such a grand scale.

In 144 ce, 60 years after their initial attempts to subdue Scotland, the Romans were still seeking to protect the empire's borders from the northern tribes. To this end, they opted to build another defensive structure, the Antonine Wall. Three metres high and with a ditch 12m wide on its northern side, this wall's sandstone foundations ran for 39 miles, between Bo'ness on the Forth and Old Kilpatrick on the Clyde. The choice of turf for the main building material would not have been practical if woodlands had dominated the environment. The Romans' other military activities did not cause widespread tree clearance either: the timber required for the camps they built in Scotland was insufficient to cause major deforestation. It has been calculated that camp construction required only the clearing of woodland three times the size of the area of the built camp. It can therefore be concluded that Scotland's postglacial tree cover had been significantly diminished before the Romans' appearance. But what had caused this widespread decline in Scottish tree cover and when had it occurred? Scientific evidence indicates the all-important order of events. Fossil pollen analysis and radiocarbon-dating confirm that permanent woodland clearance was already under way by the 5th millennium bp The hunter-gatherers' minimal impacts on the environment did not trigger permanent tree clearance: fossil pollen analysis shows that the vegetation they cleared for their camps usually regenerated. But when Neolithic farmers arrived in Scotland their activities necessitated systematic and permanent removal of turf, plants and trees.

Agriculture

Extended periods of primitive agriculture caused extensive woodland clearance. Habitats were destroyed and as minerals were leached from the exposed soil, extensive podsolisation occurred and vegetation suffered. Populations in the fertile, sheltered areas of the Central Lowlands and the Eastern Coastal Lowlands favoured an emphasis on cereal cultivation, while agriculture in the uplands tended more towards stock-rearing. It is possible that lowland and upland communities exchanged arable and pastoral products in Neolithic times: such trade was certainly well established in Scotland by the end of the first millennium of the Christian Era.

Neolithic people used stone axes and fire to remove vegetation before cultivation and to make room for their crops and herds. This clearance activity is indicated by charcoal deposits and increased proportions of grassland and cereal pollen in loch sediments.

Once the Neolithics had cleared the earth of surface vegetation, it had to be prepared for the sowing of seed. Early in the Neolithic period, people in Scotland may have used stones to break the ground for cultivation. The first purpose-built ploughs ('ards') were made of wood: some may have been made from unworked branches. Ards had no mouldboard for turning the earth over. Their function was restricted to breaking up the soil in readiness for seed-planting. As indicated by crisscross patterns visible in aerial photographs of Iron Age settlements, ards sometimes had to be used to double plough the earth at right angles. These ancient field systems also suggest that in some places spades were used as cultivation tools, and perhaps to remove turf before ploughing.

Humans probably pulled the first ards. The first archaeological evidence of ploughing implements being drawn by animals are ox-yokes like the one found in Loch Nell in Argyll and radiocarbon-dated at between c.4000 and 2500 bp.

This change to animal traction signifies a marked intensification of agricultural effort. By the early Bronze Age, in areas like parts of the southeast where humans had already cleared much original woodland cover, grass had spread. Clearing grass requires the increased power of animals to break up rooty soil. Animal traction itself demands expanded agricultural production. PJ Ashmore, in his invaluable survey *Neolithic and Bronze Age Scotland* (1996), estimates that up to half the harvest of a community's ploughed area might have had to be used to feed draught animals. Two incomplete Iron Age ards have been found preserved in peatbogs in Scotland. Numerous stone shares and tips used by prehistoric farmers to boost the ard's cutting powers have also been found; they indicate a further stage in the intensification of arable effort.

Cultivation by ard did not turn the earth over to produce permanent ridges on the soil. But as the cultivation of cereals spread (except to exposed uplands in the north and west), the division of arable land into fields began to transform the appearance of the country. The earliest field patterns were small and irregularly shaped, like those at the Scord of Brouster in Shetland where six adjoining fields occupied one hectare of ground, their boundaries marked by the stones that had been cleared to create the fields. At this period, as archaeological evidence in Shetland and Jura suggests, cereal crops were sometimes grown around individual dwellings. As agriculture developed, especially in the Central Lowlands, larger and more regularly shaped fields were established, with boundaries made by banks of stone and earth. From *c.*2500 bp the increasing use of iron ploughshares influenced the tendency to more regular field shapes.

The widespread presence of butchered cattle bones in uplands and lowlands points to the central importance of cattle for the Neolithic people and for the shape of their agricultural impacts on the environment. As well as the clearance of vegetation for agriculture and settlement, their flocks and herds significantly affected the growth of many existing plant species. The vulnerability of trees to the presence of browsing and grazing animals has serious implications for soils and, indeed, for entire ecosystems. The new domesticates were not the only animals that threatened Scotland's trees. Elk and red deer browse the tips of shoots on trees and shrubs. Deer also strip the bark from saplings and mature trees, reaching as high as three metres above the ground to do so; elk would have been able to reach even higher. However, 6,000 years ago, deer were part of an ecosystem in which they were food for the top predators – bear, lynx, wolf and humans. In contrast, the Neolithics' livestock was fed, sheltered and protected from all predators with an increasingly ruthless efficiency. As human numbers increased, the potential of their herds to modify the environment became far greater than that of any of Scotland's wild species.

Cattle do not necessarily require treeless pasture but they browse leaves and branches from trees and strip the bark from young saplings. Cattle also prevent natural woodland regeneration by trampling tree seedlings. Goats are especially destructive in woodlands: their ability to climb increases the range of the damage they do by their browsing leaves and stripping bark. Sheep do require their pasture to be cleared of trees and their grazing closely crops vegetation, restricting woodland regeneration. Sheep too will strip bark from young trees; the agility of the Neolithics' primitive sheep extended the damage they inflicted on trees, saplings and shrubs. Deforestation was caused both by the omnivorous tendencies of pigs and by their power to destroy seedlings by grubbing.

Clearly, then, the Neolithics' crops and herds were not good for woodlands and the ecosystems they contained. But can the first farmers be held solely responsible for the destruction of Scotland's original woodlands? The Neolithic population of Scotland is estimated at no more than several thousand. This small group of people using basic tools could not have stripped Scotland of her postglacial forests. Evidence from fossil pollen analysis and radiocarbon dating suggests that the moors, peatlands and bogs that replaced Scotland's original tree cover only started to form sometime between the 5th and 4th millennia bp, 2,000 years after the arrival of the first Neolithic settlers. Until that time, damaged tree cover had been able to regenerate, partially at least. Other factors must therefore have influenced tree decline apart from the activities of the first farming communities.

At this distance in time, any explanation of the reduction of Scotland's original tree cover must be approximate. Although there is still scope for wider application of fossil pollen analysis, the results of such analysis are open to varied interpretation. The decline of Scotland's original tree cover is more likely to rest on a multiplicity of factors rather than a single one. We need to know what was happening between the arrival of the Neolithics and that of the Romans 4,000 years later to discover if other factors combined with primitive farming activities to alter the non-human environment.

This period in Scottish (and European) history witnessed developments of unparalleled significance for the environment, not least the success of the agricultural way of life. With enhanced quantity and reliability of food supplies, growing populations started to make unprecedentedly marked changes in the landscape, reflecting their increasing power over the environment.

Metallurgy

The arrival of Bronze Age metallurgy skills in Scotland around 4,500 years ago represented another stage in technological development, further intensifying human impacts on the Scottish environment. Bronze is an alloy that is harder than either of its constituents. It is made by heating copper ore and tin together to produce a shiny metal, harder and stronger than any then known. The Egyptians discovered how to make bronze about 6,000 years ago. Within 3,000 years, the technology had reached central Europe and, by about 4500 bp, bronze was being produced in the British Isles, probably using copper from Ireland and tin from Cornwall. The new metal was used to make tools and ornaments. Bronze Age people buried hoards of these artefacts, probably as religious offerings. The Bronze Collection of the National Museums of Scotland shows the powerful impression bronze must have made with its strength and beauty.

Bronze could be melted by heating it in furnaces made from pottery, another Neolithic innovation. Molten bronze was cast into shapes, using moulds. It was used to make axes, knives, chisels and sickles as well as bowls, ornaments and jewellery. Bronze tools were far more efficient than their brittle stone equivalents, with bronze sickles unprecedentedly effective for clearing vegetation.

It is possible that settlers brought Bronze Age technology to the British Isles from Europe, or it may have been adopted as part of the web of culture and trade extending across the continent, itself a reflection of the material gains made by Neolithic civilisation. The two millennia when bronze was the hardest metal available to human populations in Scotland came to an end between 700–500 years before the start of the Christian Era, with the arrival of iron smelting and smithing. Iron occurs far more plentifully than do the ingredients needed for the manufacture of bronze but prehistoric smelting methods could not make a permanently hard metal from it. In the 3rd century before the Christian Era, Roman armies easily defeated Gaulish opponents, whose soft iron swords had to be re-straightened after each blow.

About 3,000 years ago the Hittites of northwest Asia Minor discovered how to produce hard iron by heating and reheating the metal before hammering it into the desired shape. Knowledge of these techniques spread through the Near East and Eastern Europe, arriving in Scotland about 500 years later.

Tools made with iron substantially increased the human population's power to modify the environment. Iron axes for clearing vegetation and iron-tipped ards for preparing soil were far more effective than their bronze predecessors. Spears with iron heads and knives with iron blades also provided far more efficient means for killing animals. Moreover, the availability of iron meant it could be used by more of the human population than the aristocratic elites who had controlled the bronze trade.

Fossil pollen analysis suggests that intensified woodland clearance took place throughout Scotland in the centuries just before the Christian Era. The Central Lowlands and the Southern Uplands seem to have experienced the widespread replacement of tree cover by cereal cultivation at the same time as iron technology became available in Scotland.

As well as using wood for fuel, expanding Iron Age populations required timber to construct settlements. Their clusters of circular dwelling structures exploited the landscape for defensive purposes: hill forts like Traprain Law in East Lothian used elevation to observe and deter attackers; crannogs were built on islands in lochs for the same purpose. In the south and east of the country, all these dwellings were built from timber and had thatched roofs; the crannogs rested on wooden piles.

On the north and northwest mainland and on the Northern and Western Isles, the relative scarcity of trees meant that stone was used to construct dwellings, notably brochs. These structures consisted of two concentric drystone walls containing stairs and galleries and supporting several wooden floors. Entrance was confined to a narrow door which could be barred from the inside. In the rest of the country, the use of timber by the growing population for dwellings and fuel impacted extensively on woodland cover. However, the technological and agricultural innovations of the Bronze and Iron Ages were not by themselves responsible for the decline in Scottish tree cover.

Climate

Fossil pollen records show that, over time, trees and plant species recovered from damage inflicted by early Neolithic farming. However, after the high point of postglacial tree growth, c.6,000 years ago, temperatures and rainfall started to fluctuate away from the climatic conditions necessary for woodland regeneration.

This trend may have been caused by postglacial meltwater submerging land joining the British Isles and the continent. The North Sea and the English Channel were formed and the entire climate of the British Isles became more subject to maritime influences, what is now the mainland being completely surrounded by sea for the first time.

The first permanent postglacial reduction in British tree cover occurred at roughly the same time as the start of Britain's island existence. Elms alone were affected. Fossil pollen analysis has shown that throughout Europe, elm cover was reduced by over half. In the British Isles, before this episode, one eighth of tree cover was elm.

In the case of prehistoric elm decline, several causes have been proposed. Pollen records date the decline at about 6000 bp, approximately the same date as evidence of the earliest Neolithic farming activity. However, fossil pollen analysis can sometimes describe the course of environmental changes better than it can explain them, and agricultural woodland clearance is only one possible cause of elm decline.

Elm was very important for the first farmers. Recognising elm growth as an indicator of fertile ground, they may have grubbed out significant quantities of the species to make room for their own crops. It has also been suggested that Neolithic farmers used ivy, mistletoe and elm branches as fodder plants. But elm disease, rather than climate or human activity, remains the most likely cause of this elm decline. The reduction of elm pollen actually appears in the records some decades after the start of agricultural activity is first indicated. It is unlikely that the small number of Neolithic people operating in Britain at that time could have achieved such a widespread reduction of elm.

The fact that elms alone suffered a continent-wide reduction in numbers suggests the trees were victims of an epidemic. Dutch Elm Disease is caused by a fungus (ophiostra ulmi), which has caused similar elm declines throughout history (its appearance in Holland in the 1940s first linked the disease with that country).

It may be that the elm's ability to reproduce through its own extensive sucker growth means that these declines are the species' management of its own sustainable development. Certainly, elm is once more on the rise in the British Isles after the species' drastic 20th-century losses. The scale and timing of the elm decline 6,000 years ago make Dutch Elm Disease a more likely cause than human activity. However, climate is too important a factor to be written out of the equation: trends in weather conditions certainly allowed the disease to flourish.

The warming trend established after the end of the last ice age continued and temperatures in Scotland held up until at least around 5000 bp. But after that point, growth of all tree species was checked by drier conditions that particularly threatened the survival of large stands of trees. Then, between 4,000 and 2,500 years ago, Scotland's climate deteriorated markedly. Year-round temperatures fell and rainfall increased. It is possible that the eruption of Iceland's Hekla volcano, c.4300 bp, was at least partly responsible for this trend, with sulphate particles in volcanic fallout blocking sunlight to reduce global temperatures. In the north and northwest especially, these new climatic conditions worked on acidic underlying rocks to cause the widespread formation of podsols and the development of heather moorland. Cool, wet conditions throughout the uplands also promoted extensive blanket bog, while raised bogs formed in many lowland areas.

These developments meant an overall loss in fertility. Trees and woodland vegetation were badly affected, especially in the uplands. Tree lines fell as species were unable to regenerate on podsolised soil or invading peat. Woodland ecosystems collapsed and animal habitats were lost, jeopardising the survival of forest dwellers like bear and lynx. Red deer, however, were able to adapt to the more open conditions.

Climatic deterioration continued and environmental damage intensified. In the two millennia before the start of the Christian Era, increased rainfall levels and reduced temperatures persisted and upland areas became increasingly less hospitable. Some palaeoclimatologists even believe the climate alone made podsolisation and peat formation inevitable in the country's uplands. In certain Highland locations such as Rannoch Moor, the overall transformation from forest to peat took place against the background of very slight human activity.

Whatever the exact hierarchy of blame for its occurrence, there is agreement that widespread vegetation decline had profound implications for all life in the Scottish uplands. Habitat loss threatened the very survival of some species, while human farming effort was significantly challenged.

Evidence from fossil pollen analysis and prehistoric field systems suggests that prior to this climatic deterioration cereal crops were grown throughout the British uplands at elevations of over 300m above sea level. But lower temperatures, higher rainfall, steep, craggy landscape and thin acidic soil together made upland cereal cultivation difficult if not impossible. The weather was too cold for the grain to ripen and heavy rainfall weakened cereal stems, making harvesting difficult.

Peat spread extensively in the Outer Hebrides, where exposure to the Atlantic Ocean exacerbated climatic deterioration. One of the most impressive Neolithic monuments in Scotland is an arrangement of 50 standing stones at Callanish on the northwest coast of Lewis. They were erected 3–4,000 years ago, at the height of Neolithic power and culture. Two thousand years later, climatic deterioration caused peat accumulation to begin and by the middle of the 19th century, over two metres depth of peat covered the stones.

By the start of the Christian Era, therefore, human and non-human factors had combined to reduce Scottish tree cover drastically. The regional situation varied considerably. In the exposed northern and western isles, very little tree cover remained. In the far northwest of the mainland, a few wooded areas survived in sheltered places and in parts of the northern Highlands there was extensive woodland with clearings. In the northern part of the Eastern Coastal Lowlands, flatter terrain had encouraged more cereal cultivation and the region was largely cleared of trees. In the central and southern Highlands, there was still extensive woodland with clearings. Trees had also been cleared for cereal cultivation in the increasingly populous Central Lowlands and the fertile south of the Eastern Coastal Lowlands; some woodland did survive in sheltered spots, however.

The climate warmed again in the first century of the Christian Era, but by then the environment of the Scottish uplands had changed forever. With soil structures irreversibly damaged by climate and human activity, moorlands and bogs were bound to spread. This meant an overall decline in fertility and the widespread and permanent loss of woodland habitat and resources, extremely significant developments for all species of upland life. In particular, human existence in the northern Highlands was greatly affected. The new and permanent poverty of the land there had a negative influence on the region's political, economic and cultural development for centuries to come. The Highlands' relationships with the Lowlands and the rest of the British Isles would be shaped by the region's multiple disadvantages – the physical barrier of the Grampian Mountains, harsh climate and impoverished soils and habitats retarded development well into modern times. However, surviving woodlands in the less heavily populated north increasingly became refuges for forest-dwelling fauna like deer, wild cat and capercaillie that could no longer survive in the more populous and agriculturally developed Lowlands.

5

On the Cusp of History

BY AROUND O CE, human populations were well established
throughout the mainland and islands of the territories that
would within one and a half millennia be known as Scotland.
Incomers had also continued to arrive from southern Britain
and the European mainland. Using Iron Age technology, these
humans had adapted to the challenges of climate change. Enough
suitable land still existed in Scotland to compensate for the loss of
upland cultivation areas to climatic deterioration. The dynamic
properties of iron blades and tips on cutting and ploughing
tools helped to clear and prepare this new acreage and the new
implements were also able to cope effectively with generally
moister soil conditions.

In fact from the Iron Age until the 18th century, Scottish
farming methods and outcomes remained essentially the same.
Iron Age agriculture featured tools and products very similar to
those of Scottish farmers 2,500 years later. Even life expectancy
did not change much over this time. Evidence from prehistoric
burials suggests that in the later Bronze Age, most people died
before they were 40: Scotland's first head-count, taken in 1755,
did not describe a longer-lived population.

Regional agricultural trade may well have been in place by the end of the Iron Age, with lowland populations specialising` in arable production, while upland communities depended more on pastoral farming. This antique division of labour and the informal exchange networks it made possible remained roughly in place until the commercialisation of the country's agriculture in the 18th century.

Though the types of agricultural impact wrought by humans on the Scottish environment remained essentially the same, the scale and intensity of such impacts increased as the country's population rose from an estimated total of $c.$300,000 at the time of the Iron Age to over one and a half million at the time of the first official census in 1801.

RJ Price, in his authoritative survey *Scotland's Environment During the Last 30,000 Years* (1983), suggests that the end of the first millennium of the Christian Era marks a key moment in the environmental history of Scotland. He identifies this as the point at which human influence over the non-human environment started to become generally more powerful than the challenges human populations faced from that environment. Such exact pinpointing of this critical stage in the evolving balance of power between the human population and the non-human environment may seem contentious. But the demographic history of Scotland during the 500 years following the first millennium of the Christian Era would seem to confirm Price's suggestion.

The 14th century's various and terrible afflictions caused a significant net reduction in the size of the human population. However, by the start of the 16th century, Scotland's population was growing again and such recovery could only have been possible from the position of human dominance suggested by Price for $c.$1000 ce, especially considering the severe climatic challenges of the Little Ice Age. By 1900 human control over that environment was supreme, thanks to the effects of agricultural and industrial development in the 18th and 19th centuries.

As well as $c.$0 ce's position en route to the human domination of Scotland's environment, the date also roughly coincides with the appearance of written documentation about the environment.

Humans inhabiting Scotland before *c.*0 ce were not literate: evidence for environmental history before this point has to come chiefly from archaeology and what scientific methods can tell us about past environments. But literacy had already started to spread through western Europe. Around 300 years before the birth of Christ, Pytheas, a merchant adventurer, journeyed from the Greek colony of Massalia (Marseilles) to explore Europe's Atlantic fringes. His record of the voyage, which may have included landfalls on the Hebrides and Orkneys, was the first written description of a circumnavigation of Britain. The original account was lost but many later influential sources, including Strabo and Pliny, cite this first written reference to Scotland's environment.

However, Tacitus's inaccurate description of an all-enveloping Caledonian Forest shows the limited usefulness of written documentation to environmental history. Yet textual evidence, treated with proper caution, can be useful – for example, documentation from the Roman empire provides useful insight into land use and farming practices. The emergence of various kingdoms within modern Scotland's boundaries and then of the kingdom of Scotland itself generated extensive written records, although many were lost to the depredations of the Vikings in the 9th and 10th centuries.

The period between the start of the Christian Era and the age of the agricultural Improvers contains two very distinctive climatic episodes: the Medieval Warm Period *c.*800–1250/1300 and the Little Ice Age *c.*1250/1300–1850 had a contrasting but decisive effect on human and non-human life, confirming the enduring significance of environmental factors in preindustrial history.

Although agricultural methods during the two millennia following the arrival of Iron Age technology changed surprisingly little, some innovations created their own environmental impacts. In the 9th century watermills and tidemills began to appear throughout the Scottish landscape, allowing farming communities to increase the efficiency of their grain processing. Another example is the arrival of guns in Scotland in the 14th century.

Hand-guns like hack-butts and demi-hacks fired 'pellocks' of lead to an effective range of 50 metres (that range had trebled by the 18th century) and they contributed to reductions in the numbers of animal species, especially those with valuable pelts.

Various human groups from outwith Scotland also had dynamic impacts on the environment. Because of their limited military success there, the Romans' presence in Scotland had few lasting effects on the environment beyond the remains of their defensive structures. But the would-be invaders did influence the development of agricultural tools and methods in the southeast of the country, where their influence and trading links were strongest. Eight hundred years later the Vikings came to Scotland as raiders. Subsequent Viking settlement in the north and the west was extensive but had limited environmental impact, for they were largely content to adopt existing agricultural practices.

In contrast, in the 12th and 13th centuries, the Anglo-Normans' feudal agenda caused significant environmental change throughout the kingdom of Scotland. The fiscal demands of an increasingly powerful monarchy required the intensification of agricultural effort including the exploitation of unproductive land; the consequent agricultural innovations and commercialisation of sheep-farming have been termed Scotland's first agricultural revolution. The Canmore dynasty's network of towns, churches, monasteries and castles also made striking and durable impacts on the landscape.

Scotland's feudal transformation owed much to the favourable climate of the Medieval Warm Period. Later, however, environmental factors helped to undermine feudal structures. Scotland's human population, despite its gradual growth, continued to rely on subsistence agriculture. Depopulation caused by the famines and plagues of the 14th century led to radical alterations in landholding practice. The last famine in the Lowlands occurred after disastrous grain harvests in the 1780s; the failure of the Highland potato crop triggered the last major famine there, in 1846. The end of famine signalled the virtual end of peasant agriculture, an essential precondition for the country's industrially-powered modernisation.

PART TWO

Environmental Effects

6

The Environment's Effects on Human Population

In 1358 on the eve of the feast of Our Lady's Nativity [7 September] flooding of rain and water suddenly burst out in parts of Lothian in such quantity and of such a kind as have not been seen from the days of Noah to the present. Its extent was such that the rising water overflowed channels, embankments and reservoirs, and spread into fields, villages, towns and monasteries. By its force it threw down from the foundations and demolished stone walls and the strongest bridges, as well as built up areas and the most substantial of houses. Likewise the violent flow dragged tall oaks and strong trees sited near rivers, uprooted by the flood water, all the way to where the rivers joined the sea. It was also responsible for removing from human use places near and far and for destroying corn that had been cut and spread out where it had been cut for drying. (Walter Bower, *Scotichronicon*)

Impacts c.0–1300 ce

CONVENTIONAL HISTORIES OF Scotland tend to treat this point in time as the beginning of recognisably important events. Human groups and their leaders are usually represented as powerful agents in historical change and the course of human progress towards familiar modernity is generally deemed inevitable. Marxist historians, who regard economic trends rather than human personalities as primary historical causes, also tend to ignore the role of the environment, which they present as a relatively unchanging and unimportant backdrop to historic, excepting major events like floods and volcanic eruptions. The effects of environmental changes that happen over longer spans of time are generally overlooked. The most momentous of these are climatic trends, such as the change from the Medieval Warm Period to the Little Ice Age, which caused severe disruptions to human society.

Climate history shows clearly just how singularly fortunate the runs of good harvests had been in the 12th and 13th centuries. Subsistence farming communities depended for survival on successful cereal harvests and thriving livestock. Invasion, tribal warfare and clan conflict could obliterate or remove harvests and livestock but in every single year of peasant farming, crop yields depended on favourable weather. Cereals could be flattened by gales, waterlogged by wet spells, stopped from ripening by cold and killed off by frost. Harvest failure triggered famine. In the 14th century consecutive years of poor harvests threatened social collapse. As late as the 18th century, the scarcity of good roads in Scotland meant that transporting grain into dearth-stricken areas was not always possible. Before the transformation of farming, famine inflicted abysmal suffering.

At the dawn of the Christian Era, the climate of the British Isles was recovering from the climatic deterioration which had occurred between c.4000 and c.2500 bp. Palaeoenvironmental and documentary evidence suggest that Scotland, along with the rest of western Europe, had been experiencing increased warmth and dryness for two or three centuries before c.0 ce and continued to do so till the beginning of the 5th century. A good proxy guide to the Scottish climate in these years is the state of English viticulture: the Romans left records showing that wine imports into England declined because a warming climate was supporting successful wine production. Wetter and colder conditions emerged during the immediate post-Roman period.

Glacial records from the Alps show two sharp periods of colder European weather, in *c*.500–700 ce and *c*.750–850 ce. Climatic deterioration caused the abandonment of coastal settlements in southwest Norway between the 6th and 9th centuries and it is possible to infer that similar pressures may have been at work in northern Scotland.

The Viking Overture

Let us brandish our swords, warrior, so that they glitter in the air; this summer we have exploits to perform.
(Egil's Saga, 10th century)

A fierce and greedy swarm of Viking raiders, explorers, traders and colonists arrived in Scotland during the 9th century. Beyond the immediate effects of their violent incursions, which regularly involved the destruction of farming settlements by fire, their impact on the environment was limited for, as already mentioned, they usually embraced local lifestyles and farming practices. Some actually used existing buildings, like the magnificent broch tower on the island of Mousa to the east of Shetland. Their voyages were very much the product of a powerful, non-human force: climate change.

The Vikings travelled the seas of the northern hemisphere from Norway, Denmark and Sweden to the Shetland and Orkney Islands, the east and west coastlines of the Scottish mainland, the Isle of Man, Ireland, England and France. They discovered Iceland, Greenland (so called to tempt future Norse colonisers) and Canada. Sailing south they reached Spain, Portugal, the Mediterranean, Istanbul, and Baghdad. From the Black Sea they sailed up the River Dnieper to Kiev, where they seized power from the ruling elite and made it an important Viking trading centre, as with York and Dublin.

This prodigious voyaging brought great material gains through trade and settlement. But the Vikings' global maritime activity was not a co-ordinated bid for conquest. Rather, it was a series of opportunistic responses to the harshness of their own native environment. Norway and Sweden stretch north into the Arctic Circle and much of Scandinavia's land surface is covered by mountains, thin soil, bog and impenetrable forests. The Scandinavian peninsula's northerly latitudes mean that growing seasons there are short, while its long coastlines are exposed to gales, salt spray, sand blow and erosion. All the region's viable agricultural land had been effectively settled well before the start of the Christian Era and by the 9th century, agricultural output could no longer feed the growing population. The resulting long-term subsistence crises forced Scandinavia's sea-warriors to set forth in search of fertile lands. Besides compelling the Vikings to undertake their mighty exodus, environmental factors also facilitated their raids and voyages over the northern hemisphere looking for treasure to loot and lands to settle: their journeying was greatly helped by the period of relatively storm-free weather that heralded the start of the Medieval Warm Period.

Western European climate change is generally foreshadowed by developments in weather patterns further north. In the 8th century, rising water and air temperatures in the northern seas meant fewer storms; Arctic ice cover also retreated, enabling the foundation of Norse colonies in Iceland and Greenland. Human life in these western colonies was only just viable and would not survive the climatic deterioration of the Little Ice Age.

As well as facilitating Viking expansion abroad, environmental conditions at home also promoted its success. Scandinavia's impenetrable interior meant that human settlements were overwhelmingly coastal and communications and trade had to be undertaken by sea. These coastal communities were perfect settings for developing the boat-building, navigation and sailing skills that underpinned the extraordinary success of Viking exploits. (One possible derivation of the name Viking is from the Norse word 'vik', meaning coastal inlet, and also the possible origin of the place-name Wick, in Caithness).

The Vikings designed highly effective boats, 'langskips', clinker-built, trim and supple, with a proper keel and a single square sail; they were capable of both extended deep-sea voyages and assaults on coastal settlements. Later on, larger versions of these boats, 'harskips', were used to bring settlers with their families and household gear to Scotland. The Vikings' maritime expertise also included the utilisation of cod, which villagers caught in open boats and preserved by drying. Cod, with its 80 per cent protein content, could also be caught and dried aboard ship to sustain the Norsemen on their long voyages.

Conquest and settlement extended the Viking sea route south past Cape Wrath (which means turning point in Norse) to the Hebrides, the Isle of Man and Ireland. Forced to explore, appropriate and colonise by powerful environmental factors, the Vikings had an immense influence on the history of Scotland. Their first landfall in Shetland became a valuable strategic base for Viking colonies from Greenland to Normandy. By 1100 the Scandinavians dominated Scotland's northern and western isles and her coasts north of the Great Glen. There were also substantial Viking settlements in Argyll and Galloway.

The cross-fertilisation between native and Viking culture shows up in the extent of Scandinavian place and personal names in Scotland: for example, almost 100 per cent of place-names in Lewis and Shetland are of Viking origin. One Viking technique with long-lasting effects was the replacement of circular building styles, common in Scotland since at least the Bronze Age, with rectangular ones. Another important Norse legacy was the udal system of land tenure, which remained in force throughout the Northern Isles until the 17th century. In contrast to the feudal regime imposed by the Canmores, under udal tenure landholders enclosed their own plot. They did not owe obligation or service to any superior and rent paid for the use of common grazings was set according to the tenants' arable holdings.

Possibly the Vikings' most important impact on Scotland's history was that their military threat accelerated the country's process of political unification. In the 9th century the most powerful native tribes, the Picts in the eastern lands north of the Forth and the Scots in the west, negotiated an alliance against the raiders. The most significant result of this pact was the emergence in 843 ce of a Scot, Cinaed mac Alpin, as first king of a unified territory. The new country would be called Alba in Gaelic and

Scotia in Latin but neither of these names was current until the 10th century.

Attempts to consolidate the nascent Scottish kingdom still had to overcome Viking power in the west and the north. In 904, Constantine II, King of Alba, defeated the Vikings at the battle of Strathearn. When Constantine retired from the throne into religious seclusion at Kilrimont Monastery on the St Andrews coast, the sea-borne Viking menace had diminished.

Continuing Viking threats further south helped indirectly to expand the territory under the control of the Scottish crown. In 945 ce Edmund, king of England, granted Cumbria to Malcolm I of Scotland in return for his assistance 'on sea and land' against the Norwegians and Danes, who were threatening to attack from their respective territories around Dublin and York. (The exact definition of Cumbria here is uncertain but probably meant the part of the southwestern mainland north and south of the modern Scottish–English Border.) The same defensive strategy against the Vikings prompted the English to withdraw from the Lothians before the end of the 10th century. When Duncan I came to the Scottish throne in 1034, his kingdom claimed to consist of Pictland, Scotland, Lothian, Strathclyde, and Cumbria. Subsequently, the monarchy gained control of more Viking lands: the Hebrides in the 13th century, Shetland in the 14th century and Orkney and Caithness in the 15th century.

Other Viking impacts were less productive for Scotland than the push to political unity. Viking raiders had first been attracted to the British Isles by the chance to loot undefended monasteries and churches. In 563 ce St Columba had founded a religious community on Iona, an islet just off Mull in the Inner Hebrides, which became the centre of the Christian Church in Scotland and Ireland. From the end of the 8th century Viking raiders repeatedly attacked the monks on Iona, taking not only gold crosses, silver cups and salvers but also women, cattle and corn. In 806 the sea-warriors extinguished Iona's spiritual light completely. They killed all 68 members of the community in a raid which gave Martyrs' Bay on the eastern side of the island its poignant name.

The continuing Viking menace necessitated moving the focal

point of the Columban church to the inland safety of Kells in Ireland and Dunkeld in Pictland. All over Scotland ecclesiastical records were destroyed by Viking raiders with the result that human history of the period c.800–1100 ce is obscured by lack of evidence.

The Medieval Warm Period

David [I] increased his power, and was exalted above his predecessors; and by his zeal the district of the Scots was adorned with religious and learned persons.
(Orderic Vitalis 1075–c.1142, *Ecclesiastical History*)

Palaeoenvironmental data and written records agree that generally warm and settled weather lasted until the first half of the 14th century. Storms and unseasonable frosts were relatively infrequent and harvest failures limited and local. Climatically induced disasters reported throughout the period include the famine that struck Holyrood in 1154 and the floods which washed away much of Perth in 1209. Trends in English wine production suggest that average summer temperatures in England were between 0.7 and 1 degrees Celsius warmer than the mid 20th century average. Unfavourable weather events did not cease entirely during the Medieval Warm Period but as sequential decades of good conditions accumulated, farmers were enabled to plan storage and estimate yields more effectively than in less climatically settled times.

Cereal cultivation was once more viable in the Scottish uplands. The records kept at Kelso Abbey show that a single one of their granges (outlying farms situated mostly 300m above sea level) grew over 100 hectares of cereals. It also kept a flock of 1,400 sheep and provided accommodation for 16 shepherds and their families. Such intensive farming activity at this elevation could only have been possible in a warming climate.

There are reports from the neighbouring Northumbrian hills of shepherds grumbling that expanding cereal cultivation was monopolising the upland areas which they wanted for grazing.

In the 12th and 13th centuries European climatic conditions guaranteed sufficient food supplies to power human industry and creativity at unprecedented levels. The continent experienced a great flowering of culture and civilisation. This was an era of magnificent building, with churches, castles, palaces and cathedrals (including Nôtre Dame, Rheims, Chartres and Canterbury) reaching new scales of grandeur and sophistication.

In Scotland the Medieval Warm Period saw the reigns of the last five kings of the Royal House of Canmore: David I, 1124–53; Malcolm IV, 1153–65; William, 1165–1214; Alexander II, 1214–49; and Alexander III, 1249–86. These monarchs enacted a policy of all-embracing political innovation in the lands where royal authority prevailed: at first Strathclyde and the Lothians and later the rest of the Eastern Coastal Lowlands, from Berwickshire to Moray, were brought under the Canmores' feudal control.

The political structures they established made radical impacts on the environment (these will be examined more closely in Chapter 11). But without the successful harvests of grain and wool and the relative ease of maritime trade provided by the more benevolent climate, Scotland's rulers could not have gathered sufficient rents and taxes to finance the vast construction projects that changed the Scottish kingdom into a functioning feudal state. Such a metamorphosis would not have been possible without the social stability ensured by two centuries of relative prosperity.

Successful feudal transformation was not just the result of a long spell of good weather; that would be far too simplistic an analysis and would ignore the importance of the personal and political strengths of Scotland's monarchy. David I was a pioneer of Scottish statehood: his modernisation programme was inspired by a mix of family tradition, fervent religion and realpolitik. His Canmore successors, especially William, Alexander II and Alexander III, pursued his policies effectively for a similar blend of reasons. But while acknowledging the importance of these human factors, it may be concluded that the Canmores' Normanisation project might well not have prospered as it did without the social and economic security provided by the Medieval Warm Period.

Impacts c.1300–1900 ce

The Canmore era was long remembered as a golden age in the troubled centuries which followed the extinction of the royal line in 1290. Walter Bower shares the prevailing tendency to explain Scotland's medieval glories in purely political terms with David I the strong, devout leader exerting his will to bring his country into the mainstream of European Christendom. Palaeoclimatologists offer another dimension to the interpretation of the 12th and 13th centuries by identifying them as part of the Medieval Warm Period. In the climatic era which followed, the Little Ice Age, annual temperatures averaged less than today's by over one degree Celsius, making it the coldest epoch since the last glaciation. The Little Ice Age lasted over half a millennium and affected Europe's human populations immensely, in ways that were increasingly documented in famine reports, trade figures and other figures kept in state archives.

The Little Ice Age: Part 1

Fluctuations occur within major climatic periods, as this chronology of the Little Ice Age demonstrates:

c.1200:   Falling temperatures in the Arctic Ocean mark the start of Little Ice Age. Economic decline in Greenland and Iceland.

1310–1320: Start of Little Ice Age in Scotland. Wet springs and autumns caused harvest failures in this decade, 1313, 1314 and 1317 being particularly disastrous years.

1500–1550: Warmer interlude of Little Ice Age in Scotland.

1550–1700: Climax of Little Ice Age in Scotland. Start of warming in Arctic Ocean.

1700–1900: Warming tendency in British Isles punctuated by temporary reversions to Little Ice Age conditions. Little Ice Age over by 1900.

Major climate shifts are made up of relative trends accumulated over time: their exact dating is a subtle and sometimes contentious process. Climate change develops at different rates in different places. In the same way that the Medieval Warm Period in western Europe was preceded by rising temperatures in the Arctic Ocean, temperature downturns in the Arctic heralded deteriorating weather. Palaeoclimatologists have traced the origins of the Little Ice Age to falling temperatures in the Arctic Ocean. These were indicated around the turn of the 13th century by the spread of ice in the seas between the Norse settlements of Iceland and Greenland. Colder conditions caused the eventual extinction of the colony on Greenland until the Norwegians began resettlement there in the 18th century.

Cooling oceanic temperatures persisted and by the second decade of the 14th century the human population in Scotland was only too well aware of the effects of these distant developments. A sharp increase in the tendency to cold and wet conditions had begun on the European mainland at the start of the century, at a time that expansion of the English vineyards was being planned, with misplaced confidence in the climate's benevolence.

During the next decade European annual growing seasons shrank by up to three weeks. From 1315 to 1321 a run of wet springs and cold summers prevented crops from ripening and harvests failed all over the continent. The cumulatively catastrophic effects of these hated 'green years' overwhelmed communities from Scandinavia to the Mediterranean.

In the Scottish countryside people ate weeds and grass and in the burghs food prices rocketed beyond the reach of all but the very rich. Beggars appeared throughout the country as successive harvest failures forced armies of peasants off the land and starvation caused disease and death among humans and animals. Bread made from unripe grain failed to nourish the populace, while animal fodder and seed for cultivation became desperately scarce. In more temperate times, communities had coped with harvest failure by swapping whatever surplus commodities they had for grain. But this was not an option during these blighted years: the impoverished peasants had nothing to exchange.

The cold, wet weather that dominated so much of the Little Ice Age made drying grain very difficult. Damp in rye-grain, a problem throughout northwestern Europe, caused an ergot blight that turned grain kernels black with toxicity. Ingesting even minute amounts caused ergotamine poisoning, known as St Anthony's Fire. Symptoms include hallucinations, convulsions and gangrene, and it afflicted the population and its livestock intermittently until the commercialisation of farming.

There were some decent harvests after the 1320s but the next two centuries were dominated by cold, wet, stormy and unpredictable weather, with the southwest winds of the 13th century generally replaced by more hostile northerlies. Peatbog evidence shows that Scotland's environment became wetter throughout the 14th century. Human livelihood in upland regions was hard hit: farming there was especially vulnerable to increased cold and moisture, as the history of cereal growing in the Lammermuir Hills of the Southern Uplands demonstrates. The upper limit of cereal cultivation on the Lammermuirs was over 425m above sea level in the 13th century. By 1600, this upper limit had dropped to 200m. During the same period, oats and rye, requiring less warmth to grow than wheat, became the most cultivated cereals in many parts of Scotland. Livestock also suffered from disease and starvation during the Little Ice Age and the difficulties of overwintering cattle were exacerbated by poor harvests.

Accompanying this disastrous decline in farming output was a long-term decline in overseas trade. During the 13th century Scotland exported significant amounts of wool, hides and woven cloth to the Low Countries. Although figures for medieval Scottish overseas commerce are sparse, the signs of a steep downturn in exports after the end of the Medieval Warm Period are revealed by customs data. In the 1430s revenues were worth only 60 per cent of their value 100 years earlier. The volume of Scotland's overseas wool trade in the last quarter of the 15th century was 25 per cent smaller than it had been in the 1320s; the export trade in skins dropped by half in the same period. Moreover, the nature of Scotland's exports changed with the climatic downturn.

The valuable trade in finished cloth dwindled and by the 16th century less valuable raw materials such as hides, wool and salt dominated the country's overseas sales. However, other factors apart from climatic deterioration also contributed to this decline in trade and to human suffering in the 14th century. The main ones were war and plague.

Wars of the 14th Century and the Black Death

> In Scotland the first Pestilence
> Began, of so great violence
> That it was said, of living men
> The third part it destroyed them;
> After that within Scotland
> A year or more it was wedand [dominant]
> Before that time was never seen
> A pestilence in our land so keen;
> Both men and bairnies, and women
> It spared not for to kill them.

(Andrew Wyntoun's Original Chronicle, c.1424)

The 14th century in Scotland has been described as one long war with England punctuated by periodic truces. In 1286, Alexander III, whose elegy opens this chapter, died suddenly and his successor, the Maid of Norway, did likewise soon after. England attempted to control the Scottish succession and for much of the next 300 years Scotland fought to retain her sovereign independence. In the Border regions, agriculture was regularly disrupted by armed violence and the armies' brutal requirements for supplies.

David I and his successors had endowed the foundation of several religious houses close to the English Border; these suffered terribly from the hostility between England and Scotland and between Scotland's nobles as they vied for control of the Crown. Successive waves of fighting inflicted severe damage on Borders abbeys, including Coldingham, Kelso, Melrose and Jedburgh. Their destruction certainly contributed to Scotland's 14th century economic decline.

Further cataclysmic disruption struck in the middle of the 14th century. As a topic in environmental history, the Black Death requires thoughtful classification. The disease, a form of bubonic plague caused by the bacillus yersinia pestis and therefore part of the non-human environment, was brought to Scotland by various forms of transport (including warhorses and merchant ships). Susceptibility to plague in Scotland was increased by climatic conditions. The Black Death had a significant effect on the Scottish environment, contributing to chronic depopulation in the Lowlands, where scarcity of tenant labour radically changed land-use patterns by the beginning of the 16th century.

The Black Death originated in Asia, where bubonic plague was endemic. Its westward progress may have been triggered by environmental factors. There was exceptionally heavy rainfall in Asia in the 1330s. Floods in China destroyed habitats and caused the dispersal of rats, whose fleas carried the plague. In 1347 the epidemic was brought to the Crimea by Mongol tribes who were besieging a Genoese trading post there. Escaping Genoese merchant ships took rats and their plague-bearing parasites to Genoa, Constantinople and Marseilles. From these busy ports the epidemic was transmitted throughout Europe where it is estimated to have killed as many as 25 million people. It reached England in 1348 on a ship that had sailed to Bristol from Gascony. Its arrival in Durham the following summer inspired the Scots to take military advantage of England's weakened condition. After inconclusive military action in autumn 1349, Scotland's soldiers returned home bringing the plague with them.

Winter conditions slowed the spread of infection but the warmth of the following spring gave it fresh virulence. Wyntoun (following John of Fordun) estimated that mortality rates were as high as one in three, but that was probably only true for the more densely populated southern parts of the Eastern Coastal Lowlands. In the north and west, low temperatures and high moisture levels slowed down the spread of the plague and generally may have meant it killed less people in Scotland than in England. However, both countries suffered from further visitations of the disease in the 1360s and '70s, and intermittently into the 17th century.

David II had been wounded and taken prisoner by the English at the Battle of Neville's Cross in 1346. He spent the next eleven years locked up in the Tower of London, effectively quarantined from the plague. Unlike the tens of thousands who succumbed to the deadly infection in London, he escaped that ghastly end.

The Black Death's contribution to Scotland's medieval depopulation was possibly not as great as that of climate change. Plague did cause some villages to be abandoned but climate-induced desertion of settlements had begun before the Black Death in the early 14th century.

The Little Ice Age: Part II

In the 15th century Scotland's climate remained cold, wet and unpredictable and the desertion of villages continued. Between 1433 and 1438 much of northern Europe suffered extensive and persistent frosts. Widespread famine ensued and there were reports of Highlanders making bread out of tree bark.

Climatic conditions reduced the agricultural viability of the uplands. Settlements emptied and a general decline in law and order occurred throughout the land. Uplander cattle raids on lowland districts increased. In the north clan warfare intensified. James I was murdered in 1436 whilst visiting Perth on the margins of the disordered Highlands. Subsequently, royal security dictated moving Scotland's permanent capital south from Scone to Edinburgh.

The Little Ice Age also caused havoc on coasts and seas. Stormy weather prevailed in northwest Europe until the 19th century, with cool oceanic temperatures continuing to cause North Sea turbulence. The sandy coasts of Holland, Belgium, Germany, Norway, England and Scotland were particularly vulnerable to this increased storminess. From c.1300 to 1800, settlements on these coasts were regularly overwhelmed by the same sort of wind-blown sandstorms which had covered Skara Brae, c.4600 bp. Peaks of North Sea turbulence occurred in the early 1400s and late 1600s.

Three events that occurred during Scotland's Little Ice Age

provide striking instances of the power of climate to control human experience. Forvie, on the east coast of Aberdeenshire, had been a settlement site since Neolithic times. A kirk built there in the 8th century was replaced by a new one in the 12th century, reflecting its growth into a thriving township. But in 1413 the settlement fell victim to a severe storm when southerly gales combined disastrously with extreme tides to shift enough coastal sands to bury Forvie under dunes 30m high.

The 1690s, a decade of extreme climatic adversity in Scotland, saw two more settlements obliterated by blown sand. In 1694, Culbin, a productive coastal estate to the west of the mouth of the River Findhorn in Moray, was hit by a violent storm. Previous heavy storms in 1663 and 1676 and the removal of marram grass for thatching might already have destabilised Culbin's sand beaches. The result of the 1694 storm was catastrophic: nine farms, a mansion and over 23 square miles of fertile land disappeared under what became known as the Culbin Sands.

This storm damage was not confined to Scotland's east coast. The Udal on North Uist, settled since Neolithic times, was by the 17th century an important dwelling place for the senior tenants known as tacksmen. In a tempest of 1697, the Udal disappeared forever under storm-blown sand.

It is worth noting that while these major storms are remembered because of their momentous and permanent effects, throughout this entire storm-ridden epoch coastal settlements all round Scotland waged a perpetual struggle to preserve productive land from encroachment by sand.

After 1500 a warmer interlude in the Little Ice Age provided respite from dearth and famine for the Scottish population, which began to increase for the first time since the end of the Medieval Warm Period. However, when cold, wet conditions resumed after around 1550, the increased population, still reliant on subsistence agriculture, experienced crisis after crisis. Harvest failures in the 1590s and 1620s caused particularly severe difficulties.

These continuing hardships provoked the start of economic emigration from Scotland. Throughout the 17th century this trend was exemplified by the numerous Scots mercenaries in the armies of European powers, notably those of Sweden, Russia and Holland. France, England and Holland were favoured destinations for civilian Scots emigrants.

In 1612 James VI of Scotland and I of England used Scottish emigration to serve two political purposes. His 'Plantation of Ulster' allowed impoverished Scots farmers to exchange their poverty-stricken farms for more sheltered and fertile lands in the northeast of Ireland. James also intended that the solid Protestantism of these emigrés would counteract Catholic threats to the English ascendancy in Ireland.

After the 1620s there were fewer runs of harvest failure and Scotland remained free of widespread dearth until the 1670s. Particularly harsh conditions prevailed in the last decade of the century. During these years, expanding Arctic ice drove Inuit kayaks south towards the Orkneys and on one celebrated occasion as far south as the mouth of the River Don.

Cold conditions at the end of the 17th century produced permanent snow cover on Cairngorm summits and throughout Scotland high-level cultivation was abandoned. Most importantly, extremely cold and wet weather through successive summers caused harvest failure in seven out of the eight years between 1693 and 1700. Upland areas were especially hard hit, with over one third of their populations dying from lack of food. The *Statistical Account of Scotland*, published in the 1790s, contained eye-witness accounts of events in Duthil and Rothiemurchus during these famine years, when 'the poorer sort of people frequented the churchyard to pull a mass of nettles and frequently fought over it...' In 1698, Andrew Fletcher of Saltoun told the Scottish Parliament that one fifth of the rural population was reduced to beggary.

This dreadful decade did not mark the very end of the Little Ice Age. In the 18th century Scotland experienced some very cold winters, particularly in the 1720s. The extremely cold winter of 1739–40, characterised by stubborn east winds and copious snowfall, saw the last wolves in Scotland exterminated after they abandoned cover in a desperate search for food. Between 1782 and 1784 the effects of a cold spike coincided disastrously with the chilling effects of volcanic fallout to produce Scotland's last general famines. By the start of the 19th century warming trends were in operation across western Europe and despite cold spikes like the ones that intensified Highland miseries in the 1840s they continued into the 20th century.

The commercialisation of agriculture and the process of industrialisation caused the wholesale alteration of much of the lowland environment over the 18th and 19th centuries. In the 19th century a marked increase in agricultural productivity guaranteed food for the industrial workforce. The success of the new techniques underpinning these agricultural advances owed much to favourable climatic conditions.

7

Wild, Wikkid Hielandmen

The manners and customs of the Scots vary with the diversity of their speech. For two languages are spoken amongst them, the Scottish and the Teutonic: the latter of which is the language of those who occupy the seaboard and the plains, while the race of Scottish speech inhabits the highlands and the outlying islands. The people of the coast are of domestic and civilised habits, trusty, patient and urbane, decent in their attire, affable and peaceful, devout in Divine worship yet always prone to resist a wrong at the hands of their enemies. The highlanders and people of the islands, on the other hand, are a savage and untamed nation, rude and independent, given to rapine, easy-living, of a docile and warm disposition, comely in person but unsightly in dress, hostile to the English people and language and owing to diversity of speech, even to their own nation, and exceedingly cruel.
(John of Fordun, 1380)

DURING THE HIGHLAND CLEARANCES, landlords throughout the north copied new farming practices from southern Scotland and England to make their estates profitable. Commercial sheep farming came to be considered ideal for the thin soils and precipitous terrain of many northern properties. For some Highland lairds, the chance of increased cash incomes justified the conflict and dispossession made inevitable by clashes between traditional subsistence farming and the new commercial methods.

The victims of these changes were the tenants, whose communities were abolished as their lands were taken over for sheepwalks. However, the extreme disregard with which Highlanders were treated during the Clearances did not start with the mass evictions of the period. It belonged to a well-established tradition of scorn, suspicion and hatred felt towards the inhabitants of the north and northwestern uplands by those of the Lowlands.

Scottish Uplands: History to 1746

'Highlander' is essentially an environmental classification. The history of the Highland region, its peoples and its relations with external powers was certainly shaped by its environment, its remote inaccessibility and relative infertility. But by the 18th century, increasingly powerful human activity was penetrating the Scottish uplands.

By this time too, the name Highlander had acquired political connotations pertaining to the five Jacobite risings between 1689 and 1745. Although Charles Edward Stewart's army reached no nearer London than the edge of the English lowlands, his attempt to seize power in 1745 provoked the British Government to dismantle the legal structures of traditional Highland society. After Culloden, military engineers continued William III's project of breaching the natural barriers which had formerly guaranteed the freedom of the Highlands from effective political control.

The isolation of some Highland populations even as late as the 18th century should not be underestimated. The mountainous region on the west coast of Inverness-shire between Loch Shiel and Loch Hourn was virtually inaccessible by land until the railway came to Mallaig in 1901. Known as *Na Garbh Chriochan* (the Rough Bounds), the area contains Knoydart, Morar, Arisaig and Moidart. Until the summer after Culloden, when the British warships HMS *Terror* and HMS *Furnace* landed troops at Borrodale near Arisaig on a mission to exact Hanoverian revenge on those who had sheltered Charles, it had been effectively independent of the state, like other extremely remote parts of the Highlands. The distant Government's red-coated soldiers had never before been seen in the district.

The upland strand of Scottish environmental history describes an extremely complex interaction of human and non-human forces. It highlights the particular challenges posed to human society by harsh environmental conditions. It also shows how those environmental conditions produced political consequences of their own, notably the early development of semi-autonomous communities in both northern and southern uplands.

By c.1400 ce material culture in Scotland's uplands was generally poorer and less sophisticated than that in the lowlands. The height above sea level of cultivable areas dropped during the 14th century, as the Little Ice Age intensified environmental pressures on marginally productive land. But long before the end of the Little Ice Age, human power over Scotland's upland environments began to strengthen, thanks in no small part to the intricate workings of dynastic politics.

Scottish Uplands, North and South

Because of the Caledonian Orogeny, upland areas north of the Central Lowlands and west of the Eastern Coastal Lowlands are dominated by the Grampian Mountains and those forming Drum Alban. The exposed situation of these northern uplands and their underlying granite and schist rocks meant that after the Bronze Age climatic deterioration, soils in much of the north and northwest of the region were generally sparse, peaty and infertile.

Communication to and from the Highlands, as within the region, was often easier by sea than land. Highlanders and their animals used tracks and pathways, may have dated back to Mesolithic times, but were certainly not suited to the requirements of organised soldiery, as the Romans found when they failed to capitalise on their victory at Mons Graupius.

From the Neolithic era, the majority of the country's inhabitants in both uplands and lowlands gained a living in roughly similar ways from a mixture of arable and pastoral subsistence farming. By the 14th century this cultural homogeneity was disintegrating. Shielings and transhumance disappeared from southern Scotland during the 13th century; at about the same time, the Gaelic language was retreating north and west, leaving Scots dominant in the south and east.

Growing hostility in lowland regions to the 'lawless' Gaelic-speakers of the northern uplands now began to appear. The diatribe by Fordun that opens this chapter typifies this animosity. These sentiments were echoed by chroniclers down the centuries, including: Walter Bower (1385–1449), Abbot of Inchcolm and royal adviser, described 'our fellow Scots beyond the mountains' as 'caterans' (marauders); Lothian-born philosopher-historian John Mair (Major) (1467–1550); and Tudor historian William Camden (1551–1623).

Captain Alexander Montgomerie, a poet in James VI's Scottish Court, sneered in verse that after fashioning a Highlandman out of a piece of horse dung:

Quoth God to the Hielandman Quhair wilt thou now?
I will doun to the Lowland Lord and thair steill a kow.

Such attitudes hardened into official persecution of Gaeldom and its alien language in the 16th century, as this declaration of James VI's clearly shows:

The King's Majesty, having special care and regard that the true religion be advanced and established in all the parts of this kingdom, and that all his Majesty's subjects, especially the youth, be exercised and trained up in civility, godliness, knowledge and learning, that the vulgar English tongue be universally planted, and the Irish [Gaelic] language, which is one of the chief and principal causes of the continuance of barbarity and incivility among the inhabitants of the Isles and Highlands, may be abolished and removed.

Environmental disparity had a lot to do with this seemingly racial hostility. Melting glaciers had deposited till in sheltered places throughout the Central Lowlands and the Eastern Coastal Lowlands, causing the development of fertile brown forest earths there. But the rarity of such soils in upland zones limited cereal cultivation and communities there had to rely on a chiefly pastoral mix of farming: it provided a poorer standard of living than that prevalent in the arable lowlands.

Upland populations were more liable than lowland ones to experience serious food shortages, especially when the cold spikes of the Little Ice Age restricted cultivation of marginal land. Uplanders intensified their use of wild food resources in times of extreme scarcity. Marine resources like fish, shellfish, seaweed and seals were especially important in famine times; whale meat was another important resource to be seized whenever the opportunity arose. Skye man Martin Martin's *Description of the Western Islands of Scotland* (1703), which gives an account of the region's culture and natural history, notes that whale meat was considered highly valuable in hard times by Hebrideans, 'particularly by some poor meagre people who become plump and lusty by this Food in the space of a week; they call it Sea Pork.' Nettles were also cooked and eaten in times of dearth and in the Highlands roots and leaves of *brisgean* (silverweed or potentilla anserina) were so highly valued that ground where it thrived was shared out formally.

Another of the uplanders' routine responses to subsistence crises was to steal livestock from neighbouring glens or from more prosperous lowland settlements; the raiders were able to evade retribution in the protective isolation of the high ground.

Such incursions were so frequent that they permanently affected the lowland psyche. Alexander Stewart, 'the Wolf of Badenoch', earned notoriety by sweeping down to harass lowland areas, perhaps from his castle at Ruthven on the edge of the Monadhliath. With his army of 'wild wikkid Hielandmen', he attacked the prosperous lowland settlements of Forres and Elgin, and burned down Elgin Cathedral in 1390.

Throughout Scotland lowlanders loathed and feared the

uplanders for their freebooting violence, extortion and robbery. Before the 17th century no political power in Scotland was strong enough to tame the uplands, whose comparative poverty offered little incentive to attempt their control. The economic self-sufficiency of most Highlands and Islands communities also helped to maintain the region's autonomy: it was not bound to the south by significant trading links until the heyday of droving.

The project by which David I and his successors sought to transform and unify Scotland through feudal government could not include all upland regions. Like the Picts before them, the Canmores had to leave much of the northern uplands outside state influence. Elgin, Inverness and Dingwall were only able to function successfully as feudal burghs because they were situated on the fringes of upland areas rather than within them. During the Medieval Warm Period, the Canmores created scores of abbeys, monasteries, burghs and royal hunting reserves in their southeastern heartlands. However, no such institutions were founded in the islands or on the mainland north of Ardnamurchan.

The Vikings dominated the western seaboard until the collapse of Norse power there in 1266. The Vikings' Gaelic-Norse successors as controllers of the region were the chiefs of Clan Donald, Lords of the Isles. James IV sent his army and navy to punish Clan Donald in the 1490s for double-dealing with Edward IV of England and subsequently the power of the Lordship of the Isles was severely diminished, but James and his successors were unable to capitalise on the clan's defeat and assert royal control over the north and northwest of the country. The resulting power vacuum reflected the Scottish monarchy's chronic political weakness.

Members of Clan Donald typified the autonomy common in the late medieval north and northwest. The remoteness of their territories on the northwestern mainland and in the Hebrides combined with their Gaelic-Norse ancestry to make them even more fiercely independent of state control than other Highland chiefs. Alexander of Lochalsh raided Lochaber and Badenoch in 1491 and ended by sacking Inverness Castle and helping himself to the town's riches. (By the late 15th century Inverness had become an important entrepôt for Highland exports, especially timber, fish and fur.)

After the demise of the House of Canmore, the strength of the Scottish crown was undermined by a variety of political circumstances. These included frequent war with England and the powerful self-interest of Scotland's noble factions as they exploited numerous royal minorities. After 1400, James I, II, III and V succeeded to the throne as children: acting as their regents, noble families like the Crichtons and the Boyds controlled royal resources and dealt with affairs of state, including international relations and the king's marriage arrangements. There was extensive scope for the regents to pursue their own selfish motives at the expense of the monarchy which was left without the power and resources necessary to exert effective authority over the country's uplands. In 1527, for instance, Alexander MacLeod of Harris was able to defy royal authority at his Dunvegan base on Skye because 'none of the king's officers dare pass [there] for fear of their lives'.

Until the 17th century royal authority was no more powerful on the high ground in the south of the country than in it was in that of the north. Although the southern hills are less substantial than the northern ones, they were still strategically significant. The elevation and bulk of the Lammermuirs, Moorfoots, Pentlands and Cheviots defended the Central Lowlands against invasion from the south and protected the regions' inhabitants from outside interference.

The border between England and Scotland that runs through the Cheviot Hills between the mouths of the Rivers Solway and Tweed had been first fixed in 1018 after the Battle of Carham (on the Tweed near Roxburgh). Malcolm II's victory over the Northumbrians restored Lothian to the Scottish kingdom and its permanent adoption was settled in 1237 (with the help of a papal negotiator) by the Treaty of York, which marked the end of Canmore ambitions to push the border as far south as the rivers Eden and Tees.

Apart from the ceding of Berwick to England in 1482, the 1237

Border has endured. Yet this frontier was never systematically fortified and at many points its exact line was officially termed 'Debatable'. Lawlessness was endemic until the 17th century and insecurity dominated life in the region, with disputes about cattle-thieving, general raiding and the exact line of the border. As Camden reported, Borderers operated according to a simple code: 'That they should take who have the power and they should keep who can.'

Taming the Uplands

Given the gradual increase in human power over the environment during the second millennium of the Christian Era, it is not surprising that the challenges of the upland environment started to be met during this period. However, a single, strictly human event brought momentous political consequences to the Scottish uplands, delivering the power of England, the strength of her army and navy and the wealth of her growing mercantile empire to the Stewart line. In 1603 Elizabeth I died without leaving a direct heir and James VI, great-grandson of James IV's queen, Margaret Tudor, succeeded to the throne of England. Regicide, republicanism and rejection lay in wait for the Stewarts. However, the Union of the Crowns, Cromwellian union (1652) and Parliamentary union (1707) each increased the ability of Scotland's rulers to overcome the difficulties the country's environment presented to effective control. Over the next century, the state's power over Scotland's recalcitrant upland populations increased.

James VI was determined to exert royal control over the boundary between his two kingdoms. In 1605, his London Government branded the border lands 'the Middle Shires' and founded a mounted force to establish order there. Two years later the laws defining Scots and English as mutual enemies were repealed and the existence of a shared monarch ended disputes over border territories. Threat of war between the two countries was over: a king could not declare war against himself.

Cross-border trade increased, especially cattle exports to England, as upland raiding metamorphosed into the commercial cattle-droving which flourished until the second half of the 19th century. This livestock trade with the Lowlands and the English lowlands expanded as southern populations grew. Droving also profited immensely from the expanding requirements of England's increasingly far-flung military commitments.

The southern uplands were better placed to benefit from these trading advantages, being less inaccessible than the Highlands. Highlanders were only able to cross the Grampians using natural access points such as the Great Glen and the Pass of Brander in the west, or the river valleys of the Dee, Don, Spey, Esk and Tay in the east. However, these ancient routes were just as unsuitable for cannons as they had been for the Roman legions and the state's firepower could not easily be brought to bear on its subjects in the northern uplands. The essential foreignness of the Highlands, symbolised by the inhabitants' much vilified Gaelic language, intensified the impression of the region's physical impenetrability.

But James VI was determined to bring the northern uplands under control. Because of the environmental difficulties posed to ordnance, his weapon against the Gaeltachd had to be social engineering. By forcing them to sign the Statutes of Iona in 1609, the king attempted to transform the clan chiefs of the Western Isles into peaceable Protestants. As well as encouraging them to relinquish their Catholicism, the Statutes urged the chiefs to restrain their followers' disorderly behaviour. In the hope of improving decorum in the northwest, the Statutes also directed them to send their sons to be educated in the Lowlands.

James did not simply disapprove of Highlanders: he was eager for the cultural annihilation of the Gaels. In 1616 his Privy Council decreed that every Highland parish should have a school to teach Highlanders to read and write in English. However, political and economic realities meant that this objective, like the rest of those outlined in the 1609 Statutes, came to nothing very much at the time,

When James died in 1625 he was succeeded by his son, Charles I, whose headstrong foolishness set the monarchy on a constitutional collision course with the Parliaments of England

and Scotland. Scotland's army played an important part in the ensuing civil wars, its prowess deriving from the influence of Scots mercenaries who had served in the Swedish army. The army fought first against Charles' forces, and then with them against those of the English Parliament.

The Royalists were defeated and in 1649 Charles was executed on the authority of the English Parliament. The Scottish army, fatally weakened by religious fervour, was unable to prevent Oliver Cromwell and his New Model Army from taking military control in Scotland following his decisive victory at the battle of Dunbar in 1650.

Cromwell's invasion of Scotland was well organised and resourced. He ruled England by military power and extended the arrangement to Scotland, forcing the country into a Commonwealth with England and Ireland, of which he was Lord Protector. He was determined to bring all Scotland under effective state control, by military means rather than by social engineering. He built forts at Leith, Perth and Inverness on the east coast and at Ayr and Inverlochy on the west; he also fortified towns and castles to establish 20 smaller garrisons, including one on Orkney.

This military network, constructed with the help of the English fleet, constituted unprecedented intrusion into the Highlands. But it was still only a limited intrusion. Forts at Inverness and Inverlochy ensured Government control of the Great Glen; but, despite superior resources and organisation, Cromwell failed to penetrate the northwestern Highlands. This impasse was lamented in frequent official complaints about the 'pestiferous burden' of the 'wilde Highlanders'. Indeed, the only royalist revolt against Cromwell's rule in Scotland was staged in the Highlands and depended on Highland manpower. The Glencairn Rising lasted 16 months during 1652 and 1653. It collapsed because of its own internal divisions, not defeat by Government forces. Cromwell's commander, General Monk, marched through the western mountains from Kintail to Inverness via Glenstrathfarrar. His comments attest to the New Model Army's struggle with the wildness of the environment:

The way for nearly five miles was so boggy that 100 baggage horses were left behind, and many other horses bogged or tired... Never any horsemen, much less an army, were observed to march that way before.

Cromwell died in 1658. Under his son Richard, the Commonwealth failed. Charles II was restored to the English and Scottish thrones in 1660. This Stewart was keen to avoid political controversy but his determination to undo Cromwell's innovations (as well as to save money) led him to reduce the number of Highland garrisons. Highland clans relished their renewed independence and the region resumed its quasi-independent status.

The death of Charles II in 1685 provoked a constitutional crisis. His brother, James VII of Scotland and II of England, was not an acceptable successor to England's ruling factions thanks to his open support of Catholicism. The English succession problem was solved when the Protestant prince, William of Orange, with his wife, Mary (daughter of James VII and II), assumed the English and Scottish thrones.

The militant Protestant ideology which welcomed this 'Glorious Revolution' was uncompromising in its fearful hatred of Catholicism. London's ruling establishment classed Highlanders as semi-criminal for their foreign tongue and their Catholicism; their Jacobitism added a veneer of heretical treason to the threat posed by the remote region where extensive coastlines could not be guarded against foreign invasion.

The original Jacobite was James VII, father of James Francis Edward Stewart, the Old Pretender. The authenticity of the Old Pretender's birth was questionable but he and his son personified the cause for which the old Highland menace once more haunted the Lowlands. The first Jacobite uprising (1688–90) followed Charles II's death. Highland forces drawn chiefly from the western clans and led by John Graham of Claverhouse, Viscount Dundee, conducted a campaign of armed resistance against William III. They won a famous victory in 1689, high in the Grampians at Killliecrankie, but Dundee was killed in the battle. The Jacobites were finally defeated by 'Loyalist' forces on the Haughs of Cromdale between the rivers Spey and Avon in 1690.

Despite this outcome, Highland Jacobite rebels, capitalising on their region's harsh and still mostly inaccessible environment, had shown how they could threaten the very survival of Britain's 'Glorious Revolution'. The northern uplands' reputation for lawless and uncontrollable disloyalty was powerfully revitalised.

The response of William III's Government to the threat of Highland Jacobitism took two striking forms. The first was enacted in January 1692, during one of the worst winters of the decade. The MacIans of Glencoe were a sept of the MacDonald clan, its medieval 'wild wikkid' identity now incorporated extreme Jacobite sympathies. The MacIans were attacked by soldiers of the British Army to punish the elderly MacIan chief for his delay in taking a compulsory oath of loyalty to William. Thirty-eight clan members were killed and more were lost in the wintry mountains. The massacre was sanctioned by the king and his chief officials in Scotland, their aim being to penalise by this brutal example the clan's open support of the Stewart cause.

The other official response to the Highlands' threat was to order the army to patrol the region more effectively. This plan impacted directly on the Highlands environment. The southern Government looked to infrastructure to neutralise the region's military threat, as Cromwell had done half a century earlier. Military engineers constructed Fort William on the site of the Cromwellian fort at Inverlochy, overlooking Lochaber and guarding the western end of the Great Glen.

William died in 1702, Mary having predeceased him in 1694. Her sister, Anne, ruled as Queen until her death in 1714. The Act of Parliamentary Union between England and Scotland was passed in 1707. Anne died without a direct heir and in order to safeguard the all-important Protestant succession, Parliament invited George, Elector of Hanover, and great-grandson of James I, to assume the British throne.

The Jacobite uprisings of 1708, 1715 and 1719 were all sponsored by France or Spain. They inspired the Westminster Government to take further defensive action against the threat that Highland insurrection continued to pose to Britain's Protestant ascendancy. The army was ordered to extend and reinforce its military network in the north: more new roads were needed for efficient movement of troops and cannon; soldiers' accommodation was also required. A number of barracks were built, including one on the site of Ruthven Castle near Kingussie and one at Kilchumein at the western end of Loch Ness.

In 1724 the Government sent General George Wade to the Highlands. As Commander-in-Chief North Britain, the Irishman's mission was the pacification of the Highlands. He started by compiling a report to George 1 on the political and military situation, summarising the problems involved in guarding the vast region against Jacobite influence, in which he wrote:

> The Highlands are the Mountainous Parts of Scotland, not defined or described by any precise Limits or Boundaries of Counties or Shires but are Tracts of Mountains, in extent of Land, more than one-half of the Kingdom of Scotland; All the Islands on the West and North West Seas are called Highlands as well from their Mountainous Situation, as from the Habits, Customs, Manners and Language of their inhabitants.

Wade thought that strengthening the Highlands' military infrastructure was essential to the region's pacification. His efforts won him national recognition, even extending to a mention in the 1745 British National Anthem:

> Lord grant that Marshal Wade
> May by thy mighty aid
> Victory bring.
> May he sedition hush,
> And like a torrent rush,
> Rebellious Scots to crush.
> God save the King!

In this context 'rebellious' was interchangeable with 'Highland': Wade was determined to improve the network of roads and garrisons to enable the British Army to counter the danger of Highlanders operating guerrilla-style from their own rugged landscape. In 1726 his engineers transformed the Kilchumein barracks into a four-bastioned fort, naming it after the nine-year-old William Augustus, Duke of Cumberland. Wade planned and built many more roads: before he left the region in 1740, he had organised the building of 240 miles of the first 'made' roads in the Highlands. Modern road-building was still in its infancy and he only had the practices of the Roman engineers to consult. Wade's roads followed straight lines wherever possible, using zigzags to climb the steepest slopes. He built a road down the south side of the Great Glen and roads linking Inverness to Perth, via Dunkeld and the passes of Slochd and Drumochter. Fort Augustus became the hub of a military network of roads and bridges. During the next 30 years his successor, Major William Caulfeild, organised the making of 800 miles of roads in the Highlands, including the crossing of the Monadhliath mountains to reach Laggan by way of the Corrieyairack Pass.

In 1745 Fort Augustus fell to the initial Jacobite onslaught. As the rising gathered momentum, Government commander Sir John Cope made the mistake of marching north from Stirling to Dalwhinnie with a small force of regulars. He could have turned west to intercept the rebels; instead, he took the safe but pointless Wade road north to Inverness, leaving the entire country open to Charles' army of Highlanders. The rebels were then able to use some of Wade's roads for their march south.

Government forces failed to prevent Charles reaching as far south as Derby, terrifying the London establishment, but this turned out to be the last time Highlanders threatened the south. Clanranald, of 'wild wikkid' MacDonald ancestry, declared his readiness to march on London with the prince, alone if necessary. One of his kinsmen lieutenants, Charles Macdonald, broke down single-handed the gates of Carlisle for the Jacobites to enter.

A campaign of violent revenge on Highland society followed. Cumberland, who arrived in the Highlands, as Cromwell had done, via the North Sea, deployed naval power to extend retribution to the west coast and his troops used Fort Augustus as a base from which to hunt down rebel sympathisers in the western mountains. In the aftermath of the uprising's defeat the triumphal British Government was determined to show it was now in control of the region and able to build effective fortifications there. To complete the Highland military infrastructure and symbolise the extinction of the Jacobite threat, Fort George – named after the new king, George II – was completed in imposing style. Considered briefly as a prison for Napoleon, it is still used as a barracks by the British Army. Taking 23 years to build and costing £200,000, the complex is enclosed in 17 hectares on the site of a medieval tower house at Ardersier Point and overlooks the Moray Firth nine miles east of Inverness. When it was finished in 1770, Fort George was the largest barracks in the British Isles. By then many Highlanders were fighting in the British Army all over the globe: the 'wild wikkid' threat had passed.

The military roads were intended to promote security rather than trade. Highlanders resented the road-builders' intrusion. They further complained that the new roads were too steep in parts, especially for carriages. Captain Edmund Burt, a military engineer, came to the Highlands in the 1720s to take part in Wade's momentous task. His letters home describe contemporary Highland life in fascinating and generally sympathetic detail. Burt classified the Highlanders' attitudes to the new roads according to their social rank. Traditional chiefs and their supporters complained that the roads would encourage the advent of outsiders whose influence would dilute the clansmen's respect for their leaders. The chiefs also feared that the roads would make their rural headquarters vulnerable to invasion: the days when traditional upland society was beyond the reach of authority were over. The Mackintosh clan held territory in the mountains south of Inverness. In 1729 Wade instructed its chief to 'desire his people not to molest my workmen.' The readiness of some Highlanders to seize new opportunities at the expense of traditional values was exemplified by those who disobeyed their clan chiefs' wishes and took the superior wages offered by the military road building gangs.

What Burt calls the 'middling sort' of Highlander resented the damage done by Wade's gravel to their horses' unshod feet; while 'the lowest class', with only 'thin brogues' or often nothing at all, had the same anxieties for their own feet. Drovers put leather shoes on their cattle before taking them on the new roads.

The Highland environment severely challenged the region's human population in medieval and early modern times: its harsh uncertainties created the 'wild wikkid hielandmen' and the lowland prejudice they provoked. After Culloden, the restrictions imposed on the powers of the clan chiefs and the outlawing of kilt, bagpipes and the Gaelic language, demilitarised Highland tribal society. Bereft of their weapons, Highlanders of all ranks were helpless to challenge the British Army's penetration of their kingless, flagless land. They were transformed from the fierce bane of the Lowlands to defeated victims, worrying about the changes threatened by the new roads. The British state neutralised the Highlands' physical defences but did not correct or compensate for the region's environmental disadvantages of remoteness and infertility. But, as we shall see, the turmoils of the '45 did not leave the Highlands with no commercial activity: pacification encouraged the adoption of Improved farming and the new roads were used by the increasingly lucrative cattle-droving trade as well as for smuggling illicit whisky south.

PART THREE

Human Effects on the Environment

8

Human Impacts in Scottish Species History

(*c.* 0 ce–1850)

The Scottes sette all their delighte in hunting and fowling.
(Holinshed's Chronicles, 1577)

SCOTLAND'S SPECIES HISTORY is difficult to chart with precision. Written documentation exists for the second half of this period but much of it is open to interpretation. Evidence from past environments is also limited. The acidity of much of the country's soil means that animal skeletons tend not to survive in great numbers; smaller animal skeletons are easily broken or dispersed. Intensive agricultural activity in lowland areas destroyed evidence of species history there and early attempts to conserve animal remains were often unsystematic. But lack of evidence and chronological certainty do not obscure the importance of habitat loss for Scotland's animals and plants, especially forest-dwelling species.

By 1000 ce Scotland contained less woodland than the rest of northwest Europe. The fertile lowlands in the south and east had been extensively cleared for cereal cultivation since the Iron Age. By the end of the Medieval Warm Period, these regions had an open, farmed landscape dotted with occasional pockets of woodland. Vegetation in the northern uplands may have been affected more by climate than clearance, though millennia of extensive grazing made a significant impact on vegetation cover there. By the end of the 18th century a tide of agricultural Improvement was transforming landscapes throughout the Lowlands.

Plant species were vulnerable. Woodland plants declined in number as tree cover diminished; some native species could not recolonise the alien environments of the Improvers' plantations. Medieval removal of peat reduced quantities of plant species including bogbean (menyanthes trifoliata), cotton grass, also called bog cotton (eriophorum angustifolium), purple moor grass (molinia caerulea), sundews (drosera) and other sedges. In the 18th century, these plants were put under further pressure by the drainage of wetlands and the Improvers' campaign to boost arable yields led to the eventual disappearance of once common agricultural weeds like corncockle (agrostemma githago) and corn buttercup (papaver hybridium).

Loss of original woodland cover had profound implications for forest-dwelling species. By the start of this period, climate change, habitat loss and human hunting had already ensured the disappearance of the auroch and the lynx. Red deer had adapted to the more open conditions but forest-dwelling species were faring worse in the more heavily cultivated south of the country than in the north. Wolves and beavers survived longer in those areas of continental Europe with more extensive tree cover than Scotland.

By medieval times wooded areas of the country distant from human influence, such as remoter parts of the Grampians, were refuges from threatened habitats elsewhere in the country. Animal bone evidence confirms that even by the start of this period, red deer and other woodland mammals were scarce in the Eastern Coastal Lowlands. The resulting shortage of game may have caused the restriction of hunting to politically powerful elites from as early as the Iron Age. Such limits on hunting were certainly in place by the 4th century.

Even curtailed hunting with bows and arrows had disastrous consequences for depleted mammal species, especially in the south and east of Scotland. Royal and baronial hunting forests were established there during the 12th and 13th centuries, to reserve game resources, especially deer, for the king and his chosen nobles. But such restrictions did not halt the decline in animal and bird numbers, a decline intensified by the extension of hunting rights to feudal landowners in the 12th century.

From at least Pictish times, dogs had been used to drive deer into elrigs. Elrigs were naturally occurring animal traps – gullies, hollows, stream-beds, or dips in the land into which animals could be driven. Elrigs were enhanced by the addition of earth or stone dykes. Traces of such improved traps survive at Hermitage Castle and at Hownam in the Borders. Where no elrig existed, armies of beaters were used to drive game to within easy range of the king and his nobles. The extreme efficiency of these killing methods significantly reduced Scotland's mammal numbers, leaving the intensively cultivated parts of the Lowlands with no more than a remnant red and roe deer population by the 17th century.

Lindsay of Pitscottie's account of James V's three-day hunt in Atholl in 1529 shows how such decimation occurred. Armies of beaters drove deer down from the hills to where the king was stationed in a specially built 'pallace' and then the killing began. The tally was extensive: 'Threttie score [600] of hart and hynd, with other small beastis sick as roe and roe-buck, woulff, fox and wyld cattis.' Such hunting spectaculars could only be staged in the Highlands after the 16th century: there was insufficient game in the Lowlands by that time.

The Scottish Parliament repeatedly attempted to revive deer numbers by legislation. In 1474 it made the unauthorised hunting of 'Deare or Raes [roe deer] in utheris closes or Parkes' punishable by heavy fines or even prison. Repeating the offence was punishable by death. At the same time, Parliament made it illegal to take deer aged less than one year old and a close season was also instituted: 'na man [shall] slaie… Raes nor Deare in time of storme or snaw.'

Continuing legal attempts to protect deer signified their ongoing decline. In the 16th century Parliament passed 11 Acts against illegal deer hunting. The appearance of guns exacerbated the problem and in 1597 the use of 'hag buttes [arquebus], hand gunnes, croce bows and pistolettes' to hunt deer was prohibited.

However, no amount of legislation could cancel out the effects of habitat loss and restore species numbers in the Lowlands: in 1682 the situation was so desperate that the temporary prohibition of all deer hunting seemed the only solution and trading in venison was outlawed for seven years.

From medieval times the Scottish fur trade also made significant inroads into Scotland's animal populations. The quality and quantity of Scottish skins and furs were celebrated throughout Europe until the 17th century. They were bought and sold at annual fur markets throughout Scotland. Boece in 1527 refers to foreign merchants buying 'furringis and skinnis' at Inverness and Ritchie (1920) makes extensive use of evidence from the Dumfries fur market. Held every February, this market sold fur and skins from Scotland's southern counties and from some of England's northern ones too. The variety and amount of animals represented in fur market data is a moving reminder of Scotland's original species roll. Animals also supplied preindustrial Scotland with many other useful commodities, such as fat, bone, skins, feathers, fibres, dyes and medicines.

Extinctions

Before the introduction of guns habitat loss was the most significant factor in animal species decline. But charting the exact process of a species' disappearance is far from straightforward and fixing the date of a species' extinction, however approximately, is also difficult. It is often hard to reconcile the extinction dates suggested by documentary evidence with scientific evidence about a species, as the case of the brown bear (ursus arctos) illustrates. The biological origins either of the bears that appear on Pictish stone carvings or of the bears that records tell us were used for public baiting and dancing in medieval times cannot be clearly established. Fossil remains confirm that bears were present in Scotland's postglacial forests but the most recent Scottish bear remains, dated to the 9th century, might not belong to an indigenous animal and so its demise may not mark the true extinction of the species in Scotland.

Determining an extinction date for the elk (alces alces) is also complicated by literary evidence. Radiocarbon dating ages Scotland's most recent elk remains at around 4,000 years old. However, Ritchie (1920) dated the species' survival to later than the 9th century on the grounds that in more than one Gaelic poem the words 'lon' and 'miol' were used at that time to refer to a swift, dark type of deer that had vanished.

Two more forest dwellers, the beaver (castor fiber) and the wild boar (sus scrofa) are reported to have become extinct sometime during the 16th or 17th centuries although, again, radiocarbon dating of each species' most recent Scottish remains gives much earlier dates for their disappearance.

Bone evidence shows that beavers were present throughout Scotland's postglacial environment. They became an important food source for the first human settlers, their bones featuring extensively in prehistoric middens. Wild boar remains have also been found throughout Scotland including in the Mesolithic middens of Colonsay and at the Iron Age crannogs on Lochlee in Ayrshire. Medieval kings hunted wild boar at Boar's Chase, near St Andrews.

Beaver and boar had more than just food value for humans. Boar hides and beaver pelts were both used by preindustrial craftsmen and skins from 'beaveris' featured in a 12th century list of Scottish exports. Beavers were also hunted from at least as early as medieval times for the pain-relieving properties of their castoreum. This mixture of beaver's glandular secretions and its urine contained high proportions of salicylic acid because of the beaver's preference for willow bark, in which the acid occurs. These multiple uses fatally compounded the difficulties habitat loss had already made for the survival of beavers and boars.

Until the use of guns became widespread, Scotland continued to be plagued by wolves, especially in less populous regions. That wolves survived in Scotland until the 18th century is generally agreed. This survival must reflect their legendary strength and cunning and their significance for Scotland's historic population is reflected in the number of wolf-related place-names like Wolfhill in Perthshire, Wolf-hole in Aberdeenshire and Wolf-gill in Dumfries.

Madadh (wolf in Gaelic) appears in several examples as in Toll-a'-mhadaidh (Wolf-hole) and Lochan-a'-mhadaidhriabhaich (Loch of the Brindled Wolf).

Traditionally, kings and nobles organised communal efforts to eradicate this marauding menace. A record survives of a 4th century king of Scots decreeing that the 'slayer of ane wolf to have ane ox to his reward'. The usual restrictions on hunting did not apply to the pursuit of wolves: anyone was allowed to kill one. Kings and nobles employed hunters charged specifically with dispatching wolves and rewards continued to be promised to anyone who killed one. The medieval Litany of Dunkeld gives us a sense of the threat wolves represented:

> From caterans and robbers
> From wolves and all wild beasts
> Lord deliver us.

In 1428 an Act of James I ordered the intensification of the communal campaign against wolves. It decreed that 'ilk [every] baron... sall chase and seek the quhelpes of Wolves... and slay them... and that the barons hunt in their baronies and chase the Woolfes four times a year.' But in 1457 the problem was still so bad that the entire population was officially encouraged to join in the wolf-hunt and the sum of a penny was promised to anyone who 'sall bring the [wolf's] hede to the sheref, bailey or barone'. By the mid 16th century wolves had been exterminated in the extensively cultivated Lowlands. However, they continued to menace travellers in wild and remote parts of the Highlands like the woods of Rannoch and Lochaber; their nocturnal howling often terrified visitors to the region.

Refuges for travellers existed throughout the Highlands and were called spittals (such as the Spittal of Glenshee on the road between Braemar and Blairgowrie). The existence of spittals was inspired at least in part by the threat of wolves. That the persistence of wolves in the Highlands symbolised the alien threat of the uplands for lowland populations is reflected in the fact that Alexander Stewart, notorious Highland raider, was dubbed the Wolf of Badenoch. Wolves were finally cleared from the Highlands in the 18th century and there are several candidates for the 'last wolf in Scotland'. Thanks to the literary efforts of the Sobieski Stewarts (claimants to the Stewart succession), tradition favours the beast killed in 1743 by its den near the head of the River Findhorn in Moray. However, the demise of any 'last wolf' was preceded by the reduction of remaining breeding populations. Such decline in the species' viability resulted from habitat loss, the general intensification of agricultural effort and the widespread use of guns.

The population of another original Scottish forest dweller, the red squirrel (sciurus vulgaris) was so severely reduced by habitat loss that in the late 18th century it was considered extinct in Scotland, although it may have been present in Speyside. The red squirrel was accidentally reintroduced into the Lowlands in 1772, when some of the Duchess of Buccleuch's English squirrels escaped from the menagerie she kept on her Dalkeith estate. Subsequently, red squirrels were reintroduced to Scotland at several locations and continued to spread prodigiously wherever remaining or newly-planted woodlands allowed. By the 19th century, the species represented a major pest for farmers and foresters.

The exact history of bird species in Scotland is even harder to determine than that of animals. This is not only due to the fragility and smallness of bird skeletons but also to the ambiguity of documentary evidence. For example, medieval reports of cranes may in fact refer to herons rather than to an extinct native breed and without scientific evidence of the presence of cranes in Scotland we cannot be certain. Similarly, Fordun reported a pair of storks nesting on St Giles Cathedral in Edinburgh in 1416 but it is impossible to know if they were representatives of a more substantial population.

The great bustard (otis tarda) was once present throughout the plains of Scotland but had became extinct in Britain by 1832. Boece refers to its presence on the Merse of Berwickshire in the 16th century and provides an excellent outline of its character and appearance:

Mukle as ane swan; bot in colour of thair fedderis and gust [taste] of thair flesche, they are litil different fra ane pertrick [partridge]... haitis the company of man... [if] they find thair eggis aindit [handled] or twichit by men, thay leif thaim and layis eggis in ane uthir place.

This description leaves no doubt about the causes of the bird's extinction: increasing human numbers and increasing human predation. Adult bustard males weighing over 20 kg made a very attractive quarry.

The capercaillie (tetrao urogallus) is a large woodland grouse that lives in pine forests. The black males are about 5kg in weight. There are numerous literary references to the 'cock of the woods' as the bird was known. It was on the menu prepared for James v during the hunting expedition referred to earlier in this chapter; in 1617, James vi hinted in a letter to the Earl of Tullibardine that he would welcome the gift of capercaillies from Tullibardine as 'the raritie of these foules will both make their estimation the more precious and confirm the good opinion conceaved of the good cheare to be had there.'

By the 17th century numbers were known to be declining and in 1621 the Scottish Parliament outlawed all trade in capercaillies, fixing the penalty for such activity at 'ane hundred pounds money'. However, in the following century comments about the bird's rarity abound, even regarding remote northern regions where it had once flourished. The capercaillie was agreed to be extinct in Scotland by 1800 and its subsequent reintroduction from Scandinavia took place in 1837.

The extensive drainage of wetlands by the Improvers and the activities of sportsmen and gamekeepers combined to cause the extinction in Scotland of bird species such as the great spotted woodpecker, the great auk and the goshawk during the 19th and 20th centuries. In the period under consideration, bird numbers generally declined due to human hunting and habitat loss.

Introductions

The concept of introduced species is problematic: species came to Scotland in a variety of different ways and as few animal species in Scotland survived the Arctic conditions of the last ice age, it can be said that many so-called native species only became native when they arrived from the European mainland in postglacial times. However, in the period from *c*.0 to 1850, human agency was most influential in species introduction to Scotland. Species were deliberately introduced for a range of human purposes or they made their own way to Scotland having first been introduced to England.

As the prehistoric arrival of the common vole demonstrates, opportunist rodents were well-suited to journey to Scotland. The original home of the black rat (rattus rattus) is thought to be southern Asia. It arrived in the British Isles sometime towards the end of the Iron Age, having taken advantage of east to west trade routes on land and sea. The house mouse (mus domesticus) probably originated in central Asia. It also appeared in Britain in the Iron Age having made the same sort of stowaway journey.

The pheasant (phasianus colchius) also originated in Asia. It was probably brought to southern Britain by Roman invaders. But according to Ritchie there are no references to it recorded in Scotland until the 16th century, when it was introduced into the Borders as a game bird.

Fossil evidence indicates that the Arctic and not the brown hare (lepus europaeus) is indigenous to Britain, as no brown hare remains predate the submersion of continental land links. Brown hares originated in Asia and their preference for open grassland meant western Europe's arable farmland offered them ideal habitats. The Romans may have been responsible for the introduction of hares to southern Britain; hare coursing is known to have taken place in Roman Gaul. The brown hare colonised Scotland, apart from the northwestern territories of its Arctic cousin.

Legislation passed in 1707, imposing a penalty of '20 pounds Scots' for anyone shooting a hare, suggests the species' relative rarity at that time. However, the expansion of cereal cultivation in the 19th century caused hare populations to expand to nuisance levels. In 1848 the legal position was reversed, allowing 'all persons [in Scotland to shoot hares] without being required to take out a game certificate'.

Fossil evidence shows that fallow deer (dama dama) were present in Britain before the start of the last glaciation but did not recolonise with the other mammals that crossed from the European mainland before the submersion of land links. Fallow deer from southern Europe may have been deliberately introduced by the Normans for hunting in the 11th and 12th centuries. In 1283 an item appears in the royal accounts for the supply of bedding and fodder for the fallow deer in the King's Park at Stirling. Fallow deer continued to be kept in deer parks and the modern population is descended from escapees.

Another Norman introduction was the domestic rabbit (oryctolagus cuniculus), which originates from the European wild rabbit. The Romans first domesticated the species for meat and fur and may have brought rabbits with them during their occupation of southern Britain. But there is no evidence of any of these surviving beyond the Roman era. Since the 5th century ce, rabbits had been domesticated in France and were bred in enclosures to provide meat and skins. As there is no evidence of rabbits in Scotland before the arrival of the Normans, today's wild rabbit population must be descended from rabbits brought to England and then Scotland by the Normans.

By Alexander II's reign, rabbit warrens were established in Scotland. Royal records from 1264 detail an annual salary of 16s 8d paid to the keeper of the royal warren at Crail in Fife. The subsequent spread of rabbits throughout Scotland is indicated by the importance of rabbit skins in the Scottish medieval fur trade. In 1424 an export duty of 12 pence was imposed on every 100 'cunning' skins and large numbers of rabbit skins continued to be sold at Dumfries until the 18th century. (The medieval word for rabbit was 'cunning' or 'coney'; rabbit is derived from the medieval word for the coney's young: 'rabettes'.)

Concluding the list of animal species introduced to Scotland in this period is another opportunist rodent, the brown rat (rattus norvegicus). It arrived in England by trading boat from east Asia in the 1720s and by the following decade was common in southern Scotland, where it eventually displaced the black rat apart from a remnant population on the Shiant Islands.

9

Farming in Scotland (*c.*0 ce–1800)

Puir laboureris and busy husbandmen
Went wet and weary draglit in the fen;
The silly sheep and the little herd-groomis
Lurkis under the lea of bankis, wodis and broomis'
And other dantit greater bestial
Within their stabillis sesyt into stall,
Sic as mulis, horsis, oxen and kye,
Fed tuskit boaris, and fat swine in stye,
Sustainit were by manis governance
On harvest and simmeris purveyance.
('Winter', Gavin Douglas, *c.*1472–1522)

THROUGHOUT THE PREINDUSTRIAL ERA all ranks of society were ultimately dependent on and involved in agricultural production. The vast majority of people lived in farming settlements and engaged in farming in order to supply their own needs. Scotland was almost entirely rural: the modern town/ countryside dichotomy did not exist until the late 18th century. The tiny settlements which were Scotland's first towns did not appear in the landscape until at least *c.*600 ce; even the burghs founded in the 12th and 13th centuries each had no more than about 1,000 inhabitants. Farming dominated those parts of the environment where it could be practised and, as already discussed, it was in areas like the Midland Valley and the Eastern Coastal Lowlands that it made the most significant impacts on the environment, impacts dating back to Neolithic times.

Continuity and Change

Despite the length of the period under consideration and the diverse conditions of the land itself, farming activities shared the same basic characteristics, whether on the waterlogged gley soils of western Scotland, the brown forest soils of the Midland Valley, the peaty mosses of the Southern Uplands and the podsolised hillsides of the Grampians. Some historians have argued for the Mesolithic origins of transhumance and the infield/outfield system. Certain practices traceable back to the Iron Age continued into the 18th century. Although products, tools and methods changed remarkably little, some technical innovation did occur and Improvers were wrong in their tendency to dismiss their predecessors as wholly conservative.

Until the 1760s farming in Scotland was generally an integrated system of arable and pastoral elements and was undertaken communally. Peasants cooperated in the tasks of cultivation and herding to supply the community's subsistence needs: food and drink, other animal products like skin and horn and whatever amounts of agricultural commodities were required for payments to the local ruling elite.

Up to the start of the 18th century most rents were paid, at least partly, in kind. The rent the people of St Kilda had to pay their MacLeod landlords, for example, included oil and feathers from the islands' vast colonies of seabirds; in the Midland Valley, rent might consist of bolls of grain or a certain number of cheeses. After money was first minted in Scotland in the 12th century, rent increasingly included payments in money as well as in kind. (The 16th century saw the eclipse of the Crown and the Church as chief landholders and the emergence of private landlords.)

By the 14th century the obligations of Lowlands tenants to

perform armed service for the lord or clan chief had been generally commuted to cash and labour service as landowners' military preoccupations waned. In parts of the Highlands, however, tenants continued to comprise the laird's fighting force and clan warfare persisted there until its bloody apotheosis in 1746.

The basic elements of Scotland's subsistence agriculture were the same throughout the country, with the balance between arable and pastoral varying according to local fertility levels dictated by the climate and geology. Arable activity was mainly concerned with growing cereal crops, and dominated the sheltered lowlands of the Midland Valley and the Eastern Coastal Lowlands. In the less fertile uplands of the north and of the southwest, pastoralism dominated. Scotland's herds were largely descended from the first Neolithic imports: cattle, sheep, goats and pigs, with strains of auroch and wild boar also present.

This pattern of mixed agriculture was probably established throughout the country by the 3rd or 4th centuries ce. The need to share land resources equitably within communities and to maximise the fertility of the land itself dictated two enduring features of pre-Improvement farming throughout Scotland: runrig and transhumance.

In the Midland Valley and the Eastern Coastal Lowlands cereal cultivation took place on rigs, the Scots word for ridges. They were created by centuries of ard, plough and spade work and provided rudimentary drainage for growing crops. Archaeological evidence confirms that some rigs were in continuous cultivation throughout the first millennium of the Christian Era and beyond.

As well as enabling cultivation, rigs also formed separate units for the system of land division, known as runrig. Runrig was one of the various forms of landholding that evolved in Scotland during this period. Similar communal land-sharing arrangements were practised in other parts of Europe to ensure a fair distribution of different qualities of land amongst tenants.

The oldest type of communal tenancy was mass tenure, by which groups of tenants held farmed land in common. Under runrig (in operation in the 12th century, though the word was not coined until the 1400s) the land was divided into individually-owned strips, or rigs. Intermingled rigs were then assigned to give tenants a share of fertile ground. Over time, a version of this system called periodic runrig developed, which regularly reallocated the strips of land. Another version, fixed runrig, involved no such reallocation. Fixed runrig was most common in the Lowlands, probably because of better overall land quality there. The final form of runrig to evolve before the demise of communal farming was called rundale. Most prevalent in the Lowlands, rundale allowed the consolidation of strips into larger blocks.

Before the era of agricultural Improvement, oats, barley and bere were Scotland's most important cereal crops. Wheat and rye were also grown, mostly in the latter half of this period; wheat could only be successfully cultivated in most favourable locations of the Eastern Coastal Lowlands, such as the Merse of Berwickshire, parts of Fife and Angus, Easter Ross and the Laigh of Moray. Until the Improvement era, wheaten bread was usually the food of higher social classes: ordinary folk only ate it on special occasions like weddings and harvest suppers. Monks in the great abbeys of the less fertile southwest, like Glenluce and Dundrennan, made their bread with wheat imported from Ireland or England.

Oats and barley were the staple food and drink crops for most of the population. Before the 18th century, oats resembled their original undomesticated species rather than today's plump varieties. Yields were much lower and, as the old rhyme testifies, peasants had various demands on their grain harvest: 'ane to graw, ane to gnaw, ane to pay the laird withal'.

Barley was crucially important as a drink crop: the ale it produced provided the medieval population's standard reviving and relatively hygienic drink. As much as one third of the subsistence barley crop was used for brewing beer. John Major praised British brewing skills and in particular the superior strength of Scottish ale. In the Highlands, barley was also used to brew beer; it was not widely used for distilling whisky there until the 16th and 17th centuries.

Cereal cultivation was only part of the community's agricultural effort. Scottish farming also involved a pastoral element which gave the country's mixed farming an annual routine based on transhumance, an ancient practice also known in the Mediterranean and the Carpathians, which involved moving livestock between upland and lowland grazing areas, according to season. Taking communal herds to high pastures maximised grazing resources: animals could feed on the summer grass of upland areas, leaving the grazing lower down to recover. Taking the herds away from the lower settlements also protected the all-important unfenced arable harvest from their incursions.

When the practice of transhumance began in Scotland is unknown but it was probably in operation throughout most of the country by the 10th century. Transhumance works well where ground is plentiful: after the 12th century this was not the case in the fertile cereal-growing areas of the Midland Valley and the Eastern Coastal Lowlands where populations were increasing. The decline of this practice started in these regions towards the end of the 12th century and was complete there by 1500. The fate of transhumance was related to the effects of the Medieval Warm Period.

First of these effects was the general growth in population numbers: more land had to be used for arable cultivation to meet increased food requirements. The food requirements of the non-food producing inhabitants of new southern burghs like Edinburgh and Berwick also stimulated increased arable cultivation.

A second source of pressure on transhumance activity in the most fertile parts of southern Scotland developed in the 12th and 13th centuries, with the appearance of new or revitalised religious foundations such as the abbeys at Kelso, Dryburgh and Melrose. The monks, taking advantage of favourable growing conditions and generous royal grants of fertile land, established some of the first commercial farming enterprises in Scotland, selling wool, grain and finished cloth to domestic and foreign customers. The monks also exploited the Medieval Warm Period's higher cultivation levels by appropriating shielings to use as outlying granges for their substantial wool-growing enterprises and so they were no longer available to the peasants for summer grazing.

Few such pressures affected the shieling system in the Highlands

EMMA WOOD

until the 18th century: David 1's feudal infrastructure of burghs
and monasteries did not penetrate the north and northwest of
the country. Transhumance continued as a central part of the
agricultural economy in the northern uplands until traditional
farming methods were virtually abolished during the years of
social convulsion remembered as the Highland Clearances.

Twentieth century Hebrideans still remembered the annual
season at the shielings being eagerly anticipated by the whole
community. Special accommodation huts were built there or
existing ones refurbished, and particular activities like spinning
and cheese-making took place. The huts' circular structures
echoed the shape of Iron Age dwellings. The men came back from
the shielings to the village without the women and children in
order to undertake annual maintenance jobs like renewing the
roofs on their houses; they also harvested their grain crops.

Innovations

The Romans never achieved complete territorial control of
Scotland but occupied parts of the south intermittently from 79
to 215 ce. Archaeological evidence indicates extensive trading
between the Romans and native tribes, especially near Hadrian's
Wall. Finds including imported and indigenous metal tools
suggest a lasting Roman influence on metalwork and agricultural
methods in southern Scotland. Iron anvils, sickles, horse-shoes,
axes, adzes and ploughshares have been discovered on sites in
Kirkcudbrightshire, Roxburghshire and Berwickshire.

The presence of two-handled scythes suggests that the Romans
may have introduced the production of hay for winter fodder.
No evidence survives to show that the Scots followed the Roman
practice of leaving a portion of arable ground fallow every year.
However, the twin Roman stimuli of superior technology and
enforced tribute influenced farming activity in the region of
Hadrian's Wall and intensified its impacts on the environment.

Before Roman influence started to operate, ploughshares fitted
to ards were made of stone and archaeological evidence suggests
that iron ploughshares were not in general use in the north until

the start of Viking settlement there. Numerous chipped-off tips of broken stone ploughshares found in the Northern Isles date from before Norse colonisation. No evidence has been found of mass violence at this time but the prevalence of Norse place-names suggests that force may have played a part in the transfer of power to the incomers. However, the introduction of iron plough fittings was almost the only innovation these successful conquerors contributed to existing agricultural practice. Norse settlers on the rocky Shetland Islands were faced with a shortage of fertile land and had to apply their maritime skills to winning a food harvest from the sea.

Possibly the earliest and most important innovation in Scottish farming during this period was the introduction of the watermill. Scotland's grain crops – bere, barley, oats and later, rye and wheat – had to be processed before they could be used as foodstuffs. Because of the damp climate, harvested grains had to be dried before being ground into meal. Small kilns, hot stones, the *tarran* (Gaelic for net-like frame) balanced over a peat fire or a hot iron griddle, were all used to dry cereals. Alexander Fenton, in his superb survey *Scottish Country Life* (1999), also mentions drying grain by graddaning. Bishop John Leslie, in his 16th century account of Scottish history and customs, describes this process of applying heat to the oat harvest simultaneously removing the chaff and drying the grain.

By the Iron Age people in Scotland were using rotary querns: more sophisticated than the simple hollow stones that Neolithic people had used, rotary querns were made from two disc-shaped stones, with a central hole in the uppermost stone into which grain was poured and ground as the top stone was rotated over the bottom one by a stick pushed into it as a handle.

The watermill took this all-important grinding process out of the domestic sphere and harnessed water power for its execution. There were two types used in preindustrial Scotland: one with the mill-wheel set horizontally underneath the mill, and one with the mill-wheel set vertically at the mill's side. Horizontal mills were first used in Asia Minor 2,000 years ago and were operating in Scotland by the 9th century ce, having arrived with settlers either from Ireland or Denmark. Engineers in the Roman empire pioneered vertical watermill technology, although the use of slaves in the empire limited the labour-saving importance of mills there. But vertical mills spread through western Europe and were present in the south of Scotland by the 12th century.

Horizontal mills tended to be smaller than vertical ones. They operated best on small, steep water-courses and prevailed in the Northern and Western Isles and adjacent mainland areas. Horizontal mills were rare in the south of the country.

The construction of mills was controversial and frequently figured in litigation. The lade, a channel which took water from a river or burn to the water wheel, had to be dug out and maintained. Dams also had to be built to cause a water flow sufficient to turn the mill-wheel. As well as the impact these installations had on the landscape, their creation and upkeep has another place in environmental history. Feudal government, greedy for dues and taxes, aimed at maximising the agricultural produce from which its revenues derived. The operation of grain mills not only made food production more efficient but also increased a landlord's ability to control and benefit from the activities of his tenants. By laws of thirlage, landowners could compel all tenants to have the grain they grew ground at the local mill. As proprietor of the mill, the landowner received multure, a fee the peasants were bound to pay for using the mill. This multure consisted of a share of the thirled peasant's ground meal; the miller was also entitled to a fee and to the peasant's labour for the upkeep of the mill and its water-sources. Querns were outlawed to maintain the peasants' dependency on the miller, whose power and wealth in preindustrial society all over Europe grew to be deeply resented.

Windmills and tidemills also existed in Scotland but the prevalence of running water there meant that watermills predominated. By the 18th century watermills were also used to power non-agricultural activities, including production of metal-ware, textile, snuff and paper.

A later agricultural innovation in this period came in the sphere of grain production and was responsible for strikingly visible effects in parts of the lowlands. At some point before the end of the 1st millennium ce, a mouldboard and a coulter were added to the ard: pivotal steps in the evolution of the primitive plough into its modern form. The coulter helped the plough to cut through the earth and the mouldboard turned the soil over to produce a ridge and furrow pattern. Crops were sown and weeded by hand on these ridges; the elevation also helped to warm up the soil. The furrows between the ridges allowed some drainage to take place, although not to anything like the extent achieved by modern, tiled drains. During the centuries of cultivating the same rigs, mouldboard ploughs repeatedly pushed earth to the top of the rigs which grew in height, sometimes to as much as three metres.

Medieval ploughs were heavy: they required teams of between two and eight oxen to pull them, numbers depending on terrain. Horses were sometimes used, taking the lead in some teams. Old rigs often have a reversed 's' shape, the result of the need to pull the ox team to the left while turning at the end of a rig in order to keep the plough cutting into the earth. Before agricultural Improvement there were no hedges or dykes to obstruct the ploughs as they turned. All each farmtoun had was a head dyke, a large earth bank built to mark the edge of the ground under cultivation. Scottish medieval ploughs were not wheeled and they were awkward to handle. While the ploughman concentrated on steering, another worker was needed to control the animal team. Extensive labour was also required for harrowing, sowing and weeding the ridges: the substantial investment in animal and human power needed for a successful grain harvest meant that the task had to be undertaken communally. Peasant communities might also own ploughs jointly.

Cereal cultivation in the southern lowlands created a specific landscape. There is scant evidence for the shape of rural settlements before medieval times but there is reason to suppose a basic continuity in rural arrangements from at least the 6th and 7th centuries ce, when many of Scotland's settlements were established.

By the 13th century the rural population was living in farmtouns adjacent to the ridge and furrow strips used by the touns' inhabitants for cereal cultivation. The farmtouns' scattered houses had dry stone and turf walls; their roofs were built from timber and covered with turf or thatched with heather. Farmtoun, like its Gaelic equivalent, 'baile', originally signified the presence of a farmstead not a town.

Throughout this period Scottish society was a sharply defined hierarchy based on control of land. Landowning elites controlled individual communities and used their own power to take rental payments from community members. These farmtoun peasants formed a sharply stratified society. Husbandmen were at the top of the tree, powerful enough to employ the services of the poorest folk to help on their holdings. Farmtouns usually contained between four and eight husbandmen and were sometimes grouped around a focal point which might give the settlement its name like Miltoun, Kirktoun or Castletoun.

Possibly as a result of feudal fiscal pressures, arable cultivation had evolved by medieval times into an efficient field system based on the intensive cropping of cereals and the manuring of crops with dung from the community's herds of pigs, sheep, goats and cattle. Arable land was divided into two distinct areas: the infield and the outfield. The infield was on the most fertile land and the peasants' houses were built closest to it. Wheat, rye, barley or oats might be grown there. In the south and southeast from late medieval times, peas and beans were also grown on the infield. These legumes were dried and ground into meal which was used to make bread. The infield was cultivated season after season, without rest. The outfield was a larger area of poorer land, only ever planted with oats. Cattle were sometimes kept on it to improve its fertility and it was not continuously harvested. The relative size of infield and outfield depended on the farmtoun's soil quality; in upland areas of marginal fertility, there might only be an outfield.

In upland regions from the Northern Isles to Galloway, generally lighter and stonier soils prevailed than in the cereal-growing regions of the south and east. But upland populations still required cereal crops and had to use cultivation tools adapted to local conditions.

Upland ploughs were lighter and cut less deeply than lowland ones. In the Hebrides, for example, the *crann-nan-gad* could be lifted or pushed across rocky ground and it cut only thin pieces of soil. The *crann-ruslaidh* (ristle), used throughout the Hebrides, was an iron blade set on a beam. It was pulled and guided through the earth like a plough but only made an initial slit in rooty ground prior to ploughing or cultivation by spade.

By the 17th century spades were also being used to prepare patches of ground for cultivation that were too small to plough. In the Highlands and Western Isles the *cas-dhireach* (straight spade) and the *cas-chrom* (crooked spade) were used to cultivate crops of oats and barley. Arduous to use, these tools were suited to the infertile region where labour was more plentiful than soil. The Duke of Sutherland, George Granville Leveson Gower, gained control of more than a million acres of the northern Highlands on his marriage in 1785 to Elizabeth Gordon, Countess of Sutherland. His schemes cleared thousands of tenants from their inland holdings to fragmented, barren settlements on the northern coasts, where they had to rely on such spades, so sparse was the soil.

Spades were also used for cultivating lazybeds on the peaty soils of the western Highlands and the Hebrides. This more intensive version of traditional cultivation, dating from the early 16th century, was a response to population growth in areas of relatively infertile soil. 'Lazy' is used here in an archaic English way, meaning that the bed was not dug over: lazybed cultivation was in fact very labour intensive. Lazybeds were created by turning over a strip of turf and then building a seed-bed on it with layers of different fertilisers, including animal dung, domestic compost and seaweed; soot-impregnated heather or turf was also added after the annual replacement of roofs at shieling time.

Some of these ingredients had to be brought many awkward miles, carried in creels, sometimes on horseback. On sloping ground, stone-retaining walls might be built around the lazybed. Until the middle of the 18th century, when agricultural Improvers popularised potato cultivation, barley was the usual lazybed crop, where it thrived in the semi-horticultural conditions.

Pastoral Farming in Scotland

Humans were intimately connected with the lives of their stock, often using their own dwelling places to house and butcher animals. Cattle provided a range of important products. There is no clear evidence for dairying in the Iron Age but by medieval times most Lowlands households outside the burghs had a cow to supply milk, butter and cheese. Beef-cattle, most common in the Highlands and the southwest, gave tallow for candles and leather for clothing, shoes and harness, as well as meat. Medieval meat consumption was restricted to the elite and may have been so since the Iron Age, given both the sharply defined social and economic stratification and the decline in available game dating from that time.

There was no fresh meat for anyone during winter months – the problem of adequate winter feed would not be solved until the Improvers introduced winter fodder crops. Animals had to be slaughtered in the autumn after the grass had died off. Beasts slaughtered at Martinmas, known as 'marts', were often used to pay the rent. Flesh was preserved in brine: the use of dry salt as a preservative was unknown in Scotland until the 17th century. An animal's offal was sometimes sewn up in its stomach bag and kept in an airtight chest – the earliest form of haggis – the name possibly being of Scandinavian origin.

The peasantry could expect none of this meat, whether fresh or salted. River fishing was also jealously guarded by monastic and other landlords. Perhaps, given the vast size of medieval sheep flocks, a bit of mutton was occasionally available; otherwise the staple diet of most people, at least in the second half of this period, consisted of oatmeal, barley, cheese and milk.

Goats, able to survive northern winters, provided the Highland peasantry with milk and cheese. After the 17th century, cattle were increasingly sold for cash to pay the rent, leaving goats as the most important food source for Highlanders. Sheep, numerous throughout the land, provided the peasantry with milk and wool rather than meat; less numerous, medieval pigs were also kept for their meat. But in the first half of this period at least, cattle retained a cultural importance that sometimes exceeded their practical value. Indicating conspicuous consumption, Iron Age evidence from Cnip on Lewis shows cattle being routinely kept on inadequate grazing and developing poorly as a result. But up to at least the 8th century, cattle predominated in Scotland's herds and the biggest proportion of meat eaten was beef.

One important advantage offered by stock-rearing was the greater ease of protecting beasts in times of conflict. Cattle, sheep, goats and pigs could be driven away to safety in emergencies, whereas attackers might burn crops where they grew, leaving a peasant community to starve.

For most of the 1st millennium of the Christian Era, Picts and Scots in the north and Britons and Angles in the south existed as warrior societies and counted their wealth in their herds. Cattle were the most valued currency. Indeed, many of the celebrated exploits of these tribal societies were based on episodes of cattle-rustling and related conflicts. Decades of Viking coastal raids in the 9th century maintained the necessity of portable resources. Such considerations applied to the entire country, at least till the establishment of David 1's feudal kingdom.

Evidence from the Northern Isles suggests fertilising was undertaken in the Iron Age by the application of animal dung, domestic waste, seaweed and wood ash. Later, throughout the country, ridge and furrow, lazybed cultivation and the infield/outfield system ensured the most efficient use of manure resources. There is even evidence of peasants being forced to keep their herds on the laird's fields so that his crops would benefit from their beasts' manure.

10

Environmental Impacts of Subsistence Society

c.0–1000 ce

SCOTLAND'S FIRST FARMING populations supported enough surplus labour to create complex societies centred on monuments such as Callanish. Agricultural surpluses continued to power social and political evolution, developments which created environmental impacts of their own. Despite the scarcity of evidence from the era between the departure of the Romans and the arrival of the Normans, some deductions can be made about that period's environmental history.

The primitive Caledonii emerged in the 9th century as the petty kingdoms of Picts, Scots and Britons. These tribes were engaged in intermittent wars with each other and in violent dynastic struggles amongst themselves. The Angles were also involved in these conflicts; they were descended from German mercenaries employed by the Romans to defend their crumbling borders. They had settled in northeast England, overcoming the Britons there.

By the end of the 9th century the Picts had lost their former territorial pre-eminence to the Scots, Gaelic incomers who had gained control of territory in the Midland Valley. Cinaed mac Alpin was the first king of the new territory, reigning from 843–858. He and his successors, notably the administrative innovator Constantine II (900–940) established effective structures for the collection of revenues, the administration of justice and the enforcement of royal authority. These Gaelic-speaking monarchs also sponsored the Celtic Church of Ninian and Columba: its prelates officiated at the kings' enthronements and blessed their armies before battle.

There were certainly plenty of battles. The emerging kingdom only survived by fending off challenges from Angles and Britons and later, Vikings and Normans. As well as fighting against these peoples for territorial control, the Scots also had sophisticated diplomatic relations with them. Constantine II allied with the Danes against the Anglo-Saxons and Malcolm III made (and broke) treaties with the Anglo-Normans.

These complex political developments depended on agricultural surpluses supporting as tribute the ruling elite, its retinue and Church. The method of revenue collection that sustained the Gaelic kingdom had its origins in the Anglian occupation of southeastern Scotland between the 6th and the 9th centuries. Tribute was gathered as the king and his entourage travelled round important settlements, such as Stirling, Scone and Dunfermline, whose surrounding areas, called 'shires', prefigured later parishes. Revenue from shires, paid in agricultural produce, was collected by the king's thane, who also supervised the use of the shire's common assets, including peat banks, watermills and grazing lands.

The thanage system, in place by the 10th century in the kingdom of Alba, was highly significant for Scotland's environment in that it methodically intensified farming effort for the purpose of paying tribute in kind. It ensured that the ruling elite was supported by the kingdom's agricultural output, thus underpinning royal control of the realm, with political power based on control of land and its produce. The success of this system depended partly on the establishment of large, individual farms capable of producing enough to supply royal demands and sustain royal representatives. Human domination of Scotland's environment by the end of the 1st millennium ce was based on growing agricultural impacts on the environment. Certainly, surpluses produced by Scottish farming and the thanage system underlay the development of the Scots' Gaelic kingdom and the many settlements that were founded between the 6th and 9th centuries.

Enough tree cover existed in the Lowlands for dwellings to be built using timber posts, with walls made from wattle and daub. Further north, stone remained more important as a building material, especially in places like Orkney where it was easy to work. The power of humans over Scotland's environment would be confirmed at the end of the Dark Ages with the relatively peaceful takeover by Anglo-Normans and the multiple and permanent transformations they wrought throughout the kingdom in the 12th and 13th centuries.

1000–1300 ce

He it is that has decked thee [Scotland] with castles and towns, and with lofty towers. (John of Fordun, of David I)

Feudalism denotes a political system based on the relationship between lord and vassal. Manorial or seigneurial are more authentic terms for feudal society, where all political identities, from that of monarch to 'neyf' (serf), were defined hierarchically by the lord's total authority over his vassal and that vassal's binding obligations to his lord.

In the 10th century Norsemen invaded northern France, where they became known as Normans: William I, conqueror of England, was descended from Rollo the Ganger (long-legged/walker), the first Duke of Normandy. Feudal structures (originating in local Frankish customs) proved highly effective means for these Viking settlers to control and exploit their new territories. Scotland's new Anglo-Norman ruling elite used the feudal system, with its rigorous control of all human life on the land and its assiduous collection of dues and taxes. This marked a distinct stage in the country's political evolution, one with unprecedented impacts on the environment.

David's father, Malcolm III, the 19th Celtic king to succeed Cinaed mac Alpin, ruled the country from 1058–93. His second wife, Margaret, was the sister of Edgar Atheling, Saxon heir to the throne of England, who had been usurped by William of Normandy's invasion of England in 1066. William did not retaliate after Malcolm's incursions into northern England in 1069 and 1070 but his hostility to Scotland increased as dispossessed Saxon nobles gathered at the Court there.

In 1072 William marched north, supported by his army and navy, and forced Malcolm to sign the Treaty of Abernethy acknowledging the Norman as his overlord. Malcolm invaded England twice more, and twice more was made to bow to Norman force and swear submission: to William I in 1079 and, the following year, to William II. The Normans responded to Malcolm Canmore's aggression by building fortifications at Newcastle in 1080.

Two years later Malcolm and Edward, one of his sons, were killed at Alnwick, campaigning against Anglo-Norman forces. His queen died three days after being told of their deaths, thanking God for purifying her soul with grief. Margaret, applauded by medieval chroniclers for her saintly piety, had been allowed by Malcolm to impose her heartfelt Anglo-Saxon sensibilities on life at his Court. She refused to learn her husband's Gaelic tongue and did her best to change what she saw as uncouth Scottish manners and religions practices. What success she had in this endeavour was made at the expense of the kingdom's Celtic traditions. David I's wholesale espousal of Anglo-Norman methods of governance may have been his mother's most significant legacy.

On Malcolm's death Anglo-Norman and Celtic powers fought for Scotland's throne. In 1094 his brother, Donald Bane, assumed control with extensive pro-Celtic support and ruled for three years. But he was Scotland's last Celtic king. With help from England, the sons of Margaret and Malcolm were able to seize the throne: Edgar, Alexander and David each ruled Scotland in turn. All of their father's energies had been spent in opposing

Anglo-Norman control: it was now ushered in by his own sons. Certainly it was family links with the English Court (his sister Matilda was married to Henry 1) which inspired and enabled David's Normanisation of Scotland.

During the reigns of Edgar and Alexander, Anglo-Normans started to take up royal grants of land in Scotland. Because of David's English connections (Henry had made him Earl of Northampton in 1114), after his succession to the throne in 1124, the northwards flow of land-hungry Norman knights like de Brus, Comyn and de Moreville increased. In return for seigniorial grants of fertile Lowlands territory, these knights became responsible for the regional implementation of David's feudal government. Each new lord's main obligations to the king were to maintain law and order in his fiefdom, be ready to muster a set number of fighting men whenever required and to boost revenues by maximising the farming output of the land under his control. The influx from England, Normandy and Flanders (northern Belgium) became a tidal wave after 1124 as David's transformation of his kingdom began to take effect. As well as knights, clerics came in search of preferment. Flemish textile workers came to run Scottish cloth production and merchants came to trade.

The strictness of feudal tax collection intensified agricultural efforts and impacts. Feudal landholders brought into cultivation so-called 'waste' – woods, heaths, moors and peat mosses, indeed any land not producing a harvest of some kind. This process was referred to as 'assarting'.

The Angles' influence is noticeable in 12th century measures to maximise agricultural yields, notably the widespread employment of estate managers and also the appointment of grieves. The efforts of these new professionals meant farming became more efficient and more land was cultivated; population numbers rose and human impacts on the environment increased.

David 1's grants of feudal tenure promoted the Anglo-Norman penetration of Scotland south of the Forth and Clyde; those of his successors, Malcolm IV (1153–65) and William (1165–1214), extended it to the north. Fife was not so extensively settled by Anglo-Normans but the native aristocracy there adopted feudal customs of tenure and inheritance voluntarily. After his successful suppression of native landowners in Moray in 1130, David colonised that region with Flemish settlers, notably Freskin and Berowald.

But there were limits to the scope of David's feudalisation programme. Royal authority was most powerful in the south and east but less secure in Galloway, Carrick, the central Highlands and Moray. Feudal power simply did not penetrate the northwest of the country: beyond Ardnamurchan, the environments of the western Highlands and Islands remained untouched by Norman influence. No royal castles were built in this area and burghs and monasteries were only established on its lowland borders. Even in regions under more effective rule, feudal principles had to compromise with Celtic realities. The native aristocracy of Atholl, significantly a part of the northern uplands, retained control of the land and maintained their own Celtic traditions of land tenure there.

Castles

The first Norman castles in Scotland acted as powerful symbols of the new feudal regime. Many were of the same defensive motte and bailey type that the invaders built as soon as they arrived in England, as pictured on the Bayeux Tapestry. These castles were constructed from timber on mottes – mounds consisting either of rocky outcrops or of raised or natural embankments up to 20m high. The bailey was an area around the base of the motte. The motte was protected by a wooden palisade surrounded by a wide, deep ditch, sometimes filled with water.

David I had witnessed the effectiveness of Norman castles in maintaining royal authority in England. He built motte and bailey castles throughout his kingdom and on its fringes in Moray and Galloway. For defensive purposes, castles were often built on boggy ground or on an island in a loch or river. The lord lived in his own wooden house on the motte and his followers lived in wooden buildings on the bailey.

These early castles were vulnerable to attack, especially by fire when besiegers used arrows coated with burning pitch. To counter this threat, layers of turf were added to the castle's roofs; walls were also plastered with clay that set hard into a less flammable covering. By the early 12th century an entire motte and bailey might cover as much as an acre.

David I also fortified the royal residence built atop the basalt volcanic plug in Edinburgh and dedicated the new castle to the memory of his mother. He improved the fortifications of existing royal castles and his imported Anglo-Norman aristocracy built castles throughout the feudal kingdom.

In the 12th century, when Scotland's few roads did not permit effective communications, castles provided convincing symbols of the power and permanence of distant royal authority. Castles were used for the administration of justice, the collection of revenues and the incarceration of miscreants. They became central to the life of surrounding communities as places of employment, entertainment, worship, imprisonment and execution.

By the middle of the 13th century wooden castles were being replaced by stone ones. The lord's wooden house gave way to a stone tower with adjoining wooden buildings for his men. These structures were enclosed by thick stone walls. The general security of feudal government established in Scotland during the Medieval Warm Period meant there was time, money and peace enough for the completion of these grander, stone buildings. Castles continued, however, to be essentially defensive structures in a land where lawless violence could erupt at any time.

Walter, head of the important Anglo-Norman Stewart family, built Renfrew Castle in 1164 and his descendants built Rothesay Castle on the Island of Bute in the following century. Like all the stone castles of the 13th and 14th centuries, Rothesay presented an impregnable stone mass, towering high above attackers with a water-filled moat in front of thick stone walls providing a further defence. The immense 'curtain-walls' often contained only a single opening, a door barred from the inside. Entry from across the moat was permitted only by drawbridge and the door itself was also protected by a portcullis. Crenellations and embrasures allowed archers to target besieging forces and defenders to pour hot oil or lead onto their heads. David I's successors built castles at various locations, including Edinburgh, Inverness, Stirling, Ayr and Dumfries. Royal castles were political strong-points administering the surrounding areas, called sherriffdoms after the new class of royal officials that replaced thanes in the royal service.

On the western seaboard and in particular the coasts of Argyllshire and Inverness-shire in the 13th century, Norse-Gaelic castle building proceeded in parallel to the Norman project. These resembled Anglo-Norman castles in their stone construction. However, they were the headquarters of maritime Norse-Gaelic lordships, quasi-independent of the Scottish throne. Clans descended from Somerled (a 12th century Norse-Gael Hebridean prince), including the MacDougalls and the MacLeods, rose to prominence after the defeat of Norse power by Alexander III at the battle of Largs in 1263. The MacDougalls built Dunstaffanage Castle and the MacLeods built Dunvegan Castle. Most western castles were enclosed by curtain walls; many were situated on sea cliffs, coastal rock outcrops, peninsulas or islands to gain prominence and protection. The building of medieval Scottish castles and fortified houses on the sites of dwellings that had been fortified since the Iron Age is suggested by the appearance of 'dun' (fortified hill) in many names, including Dunstaffanage, Dunvegan, Dunottar, and Duntrune. Archaeological excavation has proved this continuity on numerous sites, including Dun Lagaigdh on Loch Broom in Wester Ross and Dun Ringill on Skye.

The defensive strength of Scotland's stone castles was put to the test in 1296: Edward I of England invaded after John Balliol, his chosen candidate to succeed to the throne of Scotland, disobeyed commands to support an English campaign against France. Edward decided to impose his military will on Scotland as he had already done, with brutal success, on Wales.

In the face of this threat to national sovereignty, the strategic value of Scotland's castles proved very limited. First Berwick Castle fell to Edward's forces and then the royal castles at Roxburgh, Jedburgh, Dumbarton, Stirling and Lanark all surrendered without a fight; Edinburgh Castle, home of the royal treasure-house, resisted for only three days.

Edward's siege engines hurled huge rocks at Scottish castles and his miners dug under their walls, proving the tactical deficiency of 13th and 14th century castles. The effectiveness of these mighty structures had more to do with symbolising feudal authority and status than with emerging victorious from sieges.

One famous exception to this catalogue of tactical failure occurred in 1338, when Dunbar Castle successfully resisted the siege of an English army commanded by the Earl of Salisbury. Lady Agnes Randolph, wife of Patrick Dunbar, lord of the castle, was in charge of the resistance; she threw rocks at the English soldiers.

With the advent of artillery in the 15th century and the demilitarisation of Lowlands society, stone castles became outmoded and different types of elite housing developed.

Churches and Monasteries

Ecclesiastical institutions played an important role in David I's reorganisation of his country. New churches and monasteries, built of stone, symbolised the king's authority and carried his policies forward.

Christianity had come to Scotland in the 5th century and by the 7th century missionaries had taken it from the west across the mainland and islands. Saint Columba's model of communal religious life was enacted at the abbey he established on the island of Iona off the Argyll coast. Inspired by its example, in the next two centuries Columban abbeys developed at different sites in western Scotland including Lismore, Applecross, Tiree and Loch Awe. Celtic monasticism was influenced by a Christian tradition of communal withdrawal from the world; it had evolved in Egypt and Syria during the 4th century. Like their eastern prototypes, Columban communities were organised on the principal that spiritual progress could be achieved through a life of austerity, meditation and labour on the land. Echoing the desert origins of this practice, Columban communities favoured islands and other remote places; their members were also free to wander the country, preaching and converting as they went. Their religion was also shaped by Irish influences and had grown up independently of Rome. Its priests, however, were educated and cultured: many were in touch with Spain and Byzantium.

In 633 the Columban Church established itself on the east coast with the creation of an abbey on the island of Lindisfarne. Religious centres developed along the routes from Iona to Lindisfarne and the church at Dunkeld. Some of these became monastic houses, such as Inchcolm and Melrose, while some became churches like Cramond or cathedrals like Dunblane. When Viking assaults on Iona in the 9th century prompted Cinaed mac Alpin to move Columba's relics to Dunkeld Cathedral, it became the centre of a Gaelic church with its own network of parish churches and monastic communities, all housed in timber buildings.

David 1, his descendants and some of the new Anglo-Norman landowners were responsible for transforming this ecclesiastical infrastructure according to new feudal standards. Parishioners were made to rebuild their local churches in stone. In northern parts of the kingdom this church building preceded and assisted feudal colonisation: to encourage the process, sites associated with existing cults and shrines were chosen for the new churches. David also made the payment of 'teinds' (tithes) to all the kingdom's local churches compulsory for everyone who lived in the parish. This action established a legal and financial framework supporting a system of parishes which endured until the 19th century. By 1286 a parish system of over 1,000 churches had been established throughout the kingdom.

David's mother, Margaret, had supported the cults of Celtic saints like Ninian of Whithorn and Kentigern of Glasgow, the abbey on Iona and other Columban communities. But in 1068 she invited a group of Benedictine monks from the Roman cathedral at Canterbury to establish a priory in Dunfermline. Although only a small number of monks answered it, Margaret's invitation was a departure from Scotland's Celtic ecclesiastical traditions. The Benedictines had a far more dynamic and outgoing ethos than the Columbans. Margaret's descendants founded a large number of religious houses in Scotland. Her sons, Edgar and Alexander, established monasteries for Roman orders; David set up more and Malcolm IV, William and Alexander II continued the tradition. Anglo-Norman magnates in receipt of rising agricultural rents and profits also supported new monastic foundations, which were costly in materials, land and time, taking decades to complete and fortunes to finance. But there were good reasons for kings and lords to invest in these new religious communities: monastic dynamism answered the kingdom's new feudal requirements perfectly. Monks from France and England brought the culture of the European mainstream to Scotland, a culture influenced by the Christianity of Rome rather than that of the Celtic west. The religious houses set up in the 12th and 13th centuries were not just a civilising moral influence. They provided literate staff for the expanding royal bureaucracy as well as carrying out feudal principles of mercantile application. The scale of the new monks' agricultural and commercial activities was unprecedented in Scotland and their environmental impacts accordingly significant.

The monks were not merely subsistence farmers like their Celtic counterparts. Foundations like Kelso, Melrose and Dryburgh were sited on some of the best farming land in the kingdom and their agricultural efforts yielded substantial financial profits. Moreover, their proximity to the Border with England was a distinct trading advantage (in peacetime at any rate).

Among the religious orders that filled the new monasteries, the Cistercians were particularly notable for their agricultural and commercial zeal. As sheep farmers they spearheaded the development of the medieval Scottish textile trade. At Kelso, for example, the Cistercians' sheep flocks contained over 7,000 animals and they exported wool and finished cloth to England and Europe from their warehouses in Berwick. The Cistercians' interpretation of the founding rule of Saint Benedict held that idleness threatened spiritual salvation. Their consequent determination to support themselves by their own labours instead of relying on feudal dues led them to become dedicated farmers, exchanging seeds and cuttings between monasteries, working their lands intensively and bringing unproductive waste land into cultivation. The endowed wealth of the new monasteries gave them a tremendous commercial advantage. This is shown in inventories of their possessions; for example, a 14th century inventory from Coldingham Priory lists equipment, stock (including 2,214 sheep) and income from rents and teinds.

The massive commercial enterprises which the Cistercians built up over the Medieval Warm Period also benefited from the free labour of numerous lay-brothers. These monks took holy vows but their energies were used in manual or other work ancillary to the community's religious purpose. The cheap labour they supplied was a tremendous asset when it was time to sort and clean their wool in order to maximise its price. Written evidence suggests that the monks were regularly getting higher payments for their wool than other producers. Another monastic marketing advantage was the possession of carts and wagons suitable for the bulk transports necessary to fulfil profitable long-term contracts.

Monastic enterprise was not limited to farming. Monasteries at Jedburgh, Cambuskenneth, Holyrood, Dunfermline and Newbattle engaged in salt production by boiling seawater, while at Newbattle and Kelso opencast coal mining was undertaken. These activities, like its systematic agricultural endeavours, marked out medieval monasticism's highly effective exploitation of Scotland's preindustrial environment.

Burghs

There were few large settlements or towns of any sort in Scotland before David's reign. North of Hadrian's Wall, the Romans never established anything like the network of oppida that still dominated much of England's medieval landscape. Pictish society featured small, informal settlements at likely meeting places such as fords, river mouths and natural harbours. The Romans built a fort where the rivers Almond and Tay meet, just north of modern-day Perth.

Early medieval religion involved extensive pilgrimages to the shrines of native Celtic saints where enduring settlements subsequently developed. Whithorn, celebrated as the birthplace of Saint Ninian, was a destination for pilgrims from the 5th century until the coming of the Vikings. During this time, secular settlements grew up there alongside Candida Casa, possibly Scotland's first church. From the 8th century, St Andrews was an important religious centre with an associated settlement, because of the presence of the saint's relics there.

However, all these were primitive settlements; before the 12th century there had been nothing in Scotland like the burghs. These were formal trading centres and were authorised and sponsored by David I and his descendants. David initiated this policy by granting land and money for the burghs' construction and giving their inhabitants legal rights to trade and to gather tolls from passing travellers and merchants. David even employed planners like Mainard the Fleming to lay out new settlements, including Berwick and Perth, in the grid-like patterns much favoured by the Normans and still evident in these towns' centres today. David and his successors maintained high standards of design and construction in the burghs they founded, which included Glasgow, the Canongate in Edinburgh, Stirling, St Andrews and Aberdeen.

Like castles, medieval burghs were important political symbols of the kingdom's power and wealth. They were an essential part of David I's plans to bring his country up to English and European levels of commercial and cultural development; he adopted the legal regulations of Newcastle-upon-Tyne for use in his new Scottish burghs.

Burghs were a unique source of cash for the feudal monarchy. Rents from existing royal property were paid in kind but rents, taxes and tolls from the burghs were paid to the monarch in cash. David I introduced silver coinage to the country, opening mints in Roxburgh, Edinburgh and Berwick soon after his accession to the throne. Coin from the burghs was crucial to the success of his feudal project: he and his successors could use it to pay for establishing churches and monasteries.

Using trade routes originating in Roman times and extended by the Vikings into the North and Baltic Seas, Scotland's merchants brought in a range of exotic imports. Salt, pepper and spices were on sale at burgh markets, cumin being a particular favourite. Salted river and sea fish were also sold in the burghs for cash.

Much of the money required to import goods came from Scotland's exports of wool, cloth and animal hides to Europe and many burghs profited by supplying wool-growers with port and warehousing facilities.

Among the new burghs' inhabitants were immigrants bringing new skills, such as Anglo-Norman administrators and Flemish textile workers. The work of the burghs' new specialists chiefly involved the conversion of agricultural commodities into consumer goods. Leather workers produced belts, shoes and scabbards in small individual workshops often in their own houses or backyards. Wool was spun and woven, and used to make finished items of clothing. Animal horn was worked to produce vessels and implements.

This processing of raw materials was an aspect of feudal society's intensification of farming activities. Burghs, with their growing populations of non-farming residents increased the demand for grain and the surrounding countryside did not only supply craft workers with raw materials, it was also a source of labour and customers for burgh enterprises.

Houses stood on timber foundations that held upright wooden posts; these posts reinforced walls made of wattle and covered with clay and dung. Roofs were thatched with straw or heather. Risk of fire was consequently high. Kilns used for metalwork and pottery were forbidden in some burghs for that reason. Stone did not replace wood as the main construction material in Scottish burghs until the 15th and 16th centuries.

Burghs were often erected close to a castle or religious house. They provided monastic enterprises with skilled labour and with warehouses. Those like Berwick and Ayr with access to the sea benefited from Scotland's substantial export trade, especially in the closing centuries of the Medieval Warm Period; Perth profited greatly from the shipping of textile and hide exports to Europe, via the River Tay.

11

The Last Years of Peasant Farming
(1300–1846)

*Everywhere 'the plan of alternate ridges cultivated by different
farmers… anciently prevailed. As long as this injurious system
prevailed, all attempts at Improvement were in vain.'*
(Sir John Sinclair, *Analysis of the First Statistical Account of
Scotland*, 1826)

THE YEARS FROM 1300 to the 1750s were the last when subsistence
farming created the greatest human impact on Scotland's
environment. By 1600 human strength meant dynastic and
political developments could cause significant environmental
results. Responses to environmental challenges, such as the
uplands droving trade, also began to make their own marks.
Henceforth, this causal complexity prevents tracing separate
accounts of human and non-human factors. Instead, this chapter
describes pre-Improvement farming's different elements of
continuity and change and their environmental impacts.

The multiple shocks of the 14th century must have seemed
like a punishment to Scotland's human population, perhaps one
third of which was scythed down in their wake. Agricultural

effort did not cease completely under this onslaught; instead it continued in a reduced and altered fashion.

In the depopulated Scotland of the 14th and 15th centuries, landlords, including the Crown, had difficulty finding tenants and rents fell. There was a retreat from the cultivation of marginal land and in some regions farmtouns fell vacant. Although some new communities were formed, in the Lowlands overall settlement patterns changed to a more dispersed network of smaller touns.

Labour costs rose and serfdom, already waning at the start of the 14th century, had disappeared altogether by its close. The scarcity and expense of labour forced many landholders to lease property rather than farm it themselves. As a result, by the start of the 15th century, longer leases and larger holdings were becoming prevalent. These arrangements triggered the emergence of a new peasant elite in the cereal-growing regions, husbandmen who farmed between one and four oxgangs of land, an oxgang measuring about 13 acres. Eight oxgangs made one ploughgate, approximately the area one ploughman could work in a season. North of the Mounth, Pictish traditions endured and the measured unit of land for arable production was called a davoch. In less fertile northern districts the size of davochs varied.

Cottars, crofters and grassmen laboured for husbandmen as ploughmen and herds, and helped at sowing, harvest and other busy times. They rented tiny pieces of land for their huts and kailyards and were allowed to keep a few animals on the common grazing and cultivate a share of the infield. The husbandmen's superior economic position was limited by the restrictions on leases, which could last for no more than three years. But many husbandmen made the most of the new conditions and capitalised on the way labour had to be reorganised to cope with the effects of severe depopulation.

Military tenure prevailed in the Highlands until the clans were disarmed after Culloden. However, in the Lowlands feudal landholding practice in which rent was paid in kind and tenants had to render their lord military service had disappeared by 1600. At the heart of the new practices which replaced it lay the legal process of feuing. The landowning classes' growing need for cash was exceeded only by that of the Crown. These elite financial requirements were responsible for the introduction of feuing and its widespread application.

Since the reign of James II (1437–60), the Stewart family had been kings of Scotland. Royal minorities occurred repeatedly in the 15th and 16th centuries and allowed an over-mighty nobility to cause the Crown consistent political and financial weakness. Royal requirements for ready money were escalating sharply over this period as the powers and responsibilities of the Scottish state expanded in scale and complexity. Bureaucracies were established to support diplomatic activity, customs collection and the administration of justice.

New methods of waging war also added significantly to monarchical expenses. Scotland's first official reference to royal expenditure on artillery is recorded in the Exchequer Rolls for 1385 with payments made for saltpetre and sulphur, ingredients used in the manufacture of gunpowder. The 15th century Stewarts were keen to take advantage of the new weaponry and the enhanced status it promised at home and abroad. In 1430 James I imported an artillery piece from Flanders described as 'a great brass flambard'. James II used cannons in his recapture of Roxburgh Castle from the English in 1460 and was killed when one exploded during his victorious tour of inspection. The royal enthusiasm for ordnance had gigantic financial costs. To supply cannons with ammunition and manoeuvre them into battle required the permanent employment of well-trained teams of craftsmen including smiths, wheelwrights, masons and coopers.

James III and IV continued to expand Scotland's armed strength, spending further fortunes on guns as well as on the development of the Scottish Navy. James IV and his commanders, Admiral Andrew Wood and the brothers Andrew, Robert and John Barton dreamt of a fleet powerful enough to execute armed interventions in European conflicts. The King organised the construction of a flagship, the *Michael*, with which he planned to lead a crusade to the Holy Land. The wooden vessel measured 240 feet in length and its construction was said to have used up all the woods of Fife. It was completed in the autumn of 1512 but

James's life ended before he was able to fulfil his naval ambitions. He died at the battle of Flodden less than a year after the ship was finished and the *Michael* was sold off to the French who let it rot in Brest harbour.

James IV also made extravagant outlays on jewellery and opulent clothing. For his marriage to Margaret Tudor in 1503 he bought two gowns made from cloth of gold and lined with fur, which cost more than £600 apiece. He spent over £1,000 on new hangings and canopies for Holyroodhouse.

The old feudal methods of financing royal expenditure were completely overwhelmed by such demands, leaving the Stewarts in desperate need of money. The specialist labour required to operate cannons and build, sail and fight with warships could only be secured by the payment of regular cash wages. Providing such amounts of ready money was impossible for a revenue system based on feudal obligations such as supplying the king with a single archer and a sheaf of arrows for a set number of days each year.

Since the reign of David I royal expenditure had been funded from various feudal sources, including rents from the royal burghs and proceeds from the administration of justice. But the monarch, as superior lord of feudal landholders, could only obtain 'relief' in cash under certain limited circumstances, for instance when a new landholder succeeded to a property. Relief was also payable when a minor succeeded and if no heir existed to a property, it reverted to the Crown. In total, these scant opportunities represented a poor return on the Crown's vast landholdings.

The notion that the Crown should meet its own financial needs through general taxation was acceptable neither to Parliament nor to the nobility. Instead Parliament authorised the Crown to make money from its lands and indirectly from those of the Church by the introduction of feuing, a system of land tenure that paid cash to royal, ecclesiastical and noble landlords. Before the 16th century, cash was only used to pay a limited number of rents. The introduction of feuing replaced the old system's military imperatives with ones based on market considerations.

The first Parliamentary authorisation for the feuing of lands was enacted in 1458 and ratified in 1504. Two concentrated bursts of feuing activity followed, from 1508 to 1512 and from 1538 to 1542. By the end of the 17th century the feuing process had transferred the ownership of a large proportion of Crown and Church lands into private hands, providing the monarchy with some of the cash it required.

When land was feued the tenant occupying it became a feuar. A feuar had no military duties but was liable to pay an annual feu-duty, which was generally more than the former rent. A feuar also had to make a sizeable one-off payment called a grassum to the landlord for the privilege of becoming his feuar. Feuars were allowed both to sell their land and pass it on to their heirs: a market in land was established.

Feuing boosted Crown finances by making the mighty assets of the Church available to royal predation. The Crown used the menace of international heresy, symbolised by the threat of English aggression, to justify taxing the Church very heavily and the Church had to feu vast tracts of its lands to meet these demands. James v did not dissolve his country's Church, as Henry viii had done in England, but the ruinous taxes he imposed on it did lasting damage.

The commercialisation of land established by the new feuing arrangements caused significant impacts on the Scottish environment, intensifying as it did humans' need to exploit to the maximum degree whatever land they held. All land became part of the cash economy and was made to render its maximum monetary value. Feuars were under pressure to make enough money from their lands to cover costs of grassum and annual feu-duties. In addition, feuars also had to execute improvement plans agreed with the landlord when the feu commenced. These might include construction of new buildings, cultivation of waste land, tree-planting and the addition of useful features like dovecots, fish hatcheries and rabbit warrens. The feuars' heritable tenure provided the incentive for such improvements. Although feuing affected different regions of Scotland in different socio-economic ways, in general it intensified human impacts on the environment.

The advent of absentee landlords was another direct result of the introduction of feuing. These first absentee landlords were often members of the merchant class and the legal profession; they were cash investors in land but not working inhabitants of the property they owned and they symbolised the new commercialisation of Scottish landholding.

16th century trends towards demilitarisation of Lowlands society were reflected in changing designs for elite housing. Lairds' dwellings were increasingly constructed with display rather than defence in mind. Three-storey tower houses replaced castles during the 15th century. General scarcity of timber, especially in the populous cereal-growing regions, meant they were built from stone. They featured crenellations and corbelled turrets, symbolic reminders of former defences as well as assertions of noble status.

As the importance of military concerns continued to recede, the vertical style of tower houses was replaced by a horizontal one. Interiors became more sumptuous, with a greater stress on the laird's privacy and convenience, as with the transformation in 1460 of Huntly Castle into the House of Strathbogie. Scottish building styles were affected by various foreign influences including Dutch and Italian. Marie de Guise's decade and a half of power as Scottish Queen and Regent inspired a lasting French influence. Timothy Pont, a late 16th century son of the manse, made the first known detailed maps of Scotland. One of the surviving 77 Pont maps shows impressive Renaissance buildings on the Clyde reminiscent of similar developments on the Loire.

Architectural changes were also prompted by the arrival of artillery in Scotland as royal castles at Stirling, Dumbarton and Edinburgh were redesigned to meet the new challenges, their curtain walls replaced by heavier structures and cannon emplacements and casemates added to house new defensive firepower.

In 1603 Regal Union with England and the resulting pacification of the Borders fostered an increased sense of security throughout the Lowlands. This encouraged activity on the land and in commerce as the Union itself increased trade with England.

In the Lowlands, a richer class of peasants took possession of medium-sized properties feued in the 16th century. However, after 1600, falling grain profits and rising land values forced them to sell out to wealthier lairds who were thus able to acquire larger holdings and form a new, 'middling' class of landowners, who were less and less concerned than their predecessors with armed strength and readiness for battle. After 1603, the lairds' energies were increasingly devoted to getting and spending the fruits of Scotland's expanding cash economy, a development with immense implications for the environment over the coming centuries.

The demilitarisation of Lowlands society continued to affect the evolution of the region's architecture. No fortified house was built in the Lowlands after the 1660s; instead, the region saw the building of more and more stately, horizontal houses, as happened on the sites of Arniston House (Lothian) and Finlaystone House (Strathclyde). Designed by Scotland's first professional architects, according to chivalric rather than defensive principles, these new buildings reflected the decline in regular local warfare. They also displayed landowners' growing interest in material comforts: well-furnished interiors became as important as commanding exteriors.

Until the middle of the 18th century the vast majority of these new buildings stood in an unchanged rural landscape dominated by unfenced blocks of rigs separated by weed-covered earth banks; the general treelessness of the Lowlands at the start of the 17th century is recorded on Pont's maps.

Some progressive trends were at work in the Scottish countryside. Individual innovations were being made in 17th century Scottish farming, most notably in the Lothians and Berwickshire, where thriving grain markets exerted a progressive influence. There is literary evidence of contemporary Scottish interest in agricultural Improvement. John Skene of Hallyards in Kirkliston, East Lothian, wrote his notes 'On Husbandrie' in the 1660s. The country's terrible experiences of famine in the 1690s inspired a national sense of concern about Scottish agriculture. James Donaldson and Lord Belhaven were among those who published their recommendations for profitable farming reform.

The modernising influence of Scotland's cash economy was not confined to the cereal-growing Lowlands. The droving of cattle from the Scottish uplands for sale to graziers in the Lowlands and England continued to flourish, becoming one of Scotland's most valuable exports in the 17th and 18th centuries.

After 1600 there was a rising demand for meat in Scottish and English towns but, until the pacification of the Highlands which followed Culloden, English cattle dealers were afraid to come north. Droving cattle south solved this difficulty. The droving trade was also the perfect solution to harsh upland climates: once the grass stopped growing in the autumn, upland cattle were doomed to starve. Root crops and hay would not close this hungry gap in Scottish farming until the Improvers' innovations.

The drovers' herds of black cattle – kyloes from the west and norlands from the north – were direct descendants of the cattle brought to Scotland by Neolithic incomers. The animals lost condition on their long journeys south and had to be restored by grazing in pastures closer to their destinations. Traditionally, tenants reared black cattle to pay their rent and goats to provide their own milk and wool.

But in contrast to the valuable cash rewards earned by droving, the trade caused an overall degradation of upland environments. The export of livestock effectively removed nitrogen, calcium and organic matter from upland ecosystems without replacing them.

The drovers and their charges created their own tracks down to the Lowlands; these, until General Wade's roads, formed the Highlands' main communication network. When Thomas Telford began working for the Commissioners of Highland Roads and Bridges at the start of the 19th century, he described Highland roads before Wade as 'merely the tracks of black cattle and horses intersected by numerous rapid streams which being frequently swollen into torrents by heavy rains rendered them dangerous or impassable'. Wade's engineers followed some drovers' tracks in the Monaliadh but in many parts of the uplands the trails left by the drovers' convoys took neither the straightest nor shortest routes. Drovers preferred making their way through open country.

Guiding their charges on foot or, less often, on ponies, these hardy men were accustomed by the demands of upland conditions to lives judged by observers to be both 'hazardous and fatiguing'. They led hundreds of beasts at a time along routes decided by weather and ground conditions. The stream of cows spread out as widely as it could, like water, with each animal reluctant to tread where the ground had been broken by the ones in front. The droves moved between ten and twelve miles daily with an hour's rest at midday. They spent each night at stances, ideally sheltered spots with grazing.

Cattle raised on rough upland grazing took four or five years to grow big enough to be sold (at about 135kg). The drovers walked them to lowland fairs like Dumfries in the southwest and Muir of Ord and Crieff in the north. Cattle from the Scottish uplands might be walked as far as the Norfolk marshes to be fattened for the London market.

To reach mainland markets animals were swum from Hebridean islands and across mainland rivers. Government provision of ferries and bridges in the 18th and 19th centuries ended this practice. Drovers, however, did not always welcome the new bridges: their narrowness and noise could easily panic cattle, especially beasts fresh from the summer grazings.

Lowland farmers were upset when drovers' cattle strayed into growing crops. As the droving trade expanded in the southwest, earth dykes were built to safeguard arable land there. The droving trade also antagonised the 17th century Scottish Government: in times of food scarcity, the authorities attempted to restrict the export of foodstuffs from Scotland, forcing the drovers to resort to evasive tactics.

The Regal Union did not immediately help the drovers: they still had tolls to pay when they crossed the Border and the pacification of that region did not come about at once. But the power of England's growing demand for meat was enough to counter these difficulties. By the middle of the 17th century the droving trade with England was so important that, according to ARB Haldane's excellent account (1952), Scotland was increasingly seen as England's grazing field. After the 1660s, tolls on the droving trade were relaxed. Scotland's Privy Council, seeking to boost the national income, was actively encouraging cattle exports by the end of the century.

Droving did not bring prosperity to all the uplands' inhabitants. Conditions for most there meant subsistence livelihoods were hard-won and precarious. Upland communities had few options if harvest or livestock failed. In 1680, the 30-strong population of the northerly Hebridean island of North Rona died of starvation after a plague of rats ate their store of meal. Their fate shows how close starvation was for many Highland communities. Visitors to the Highlands frequently commented on the material poverty of the region's inhabitants.

Further south, the decades around the turn of the 18th century saw important political developments which encouraged progressive trends in Scotland's agriculture. The 'Glorious Revolution' of 1688 averted the threat of religious civil war and made possible the pacification of the Lowlands and of those parts of Scotland unaffected by Jacobite influence.

James II's youngest daughter, Anne, succeeded to the throne in 1702. Five years later she assented to the Acts passed by the English and Scottish Parliaments confirming Parliamentary Union. The motives of the Westminster establishment were very much to do with securing the extensive coastline of 'North Britain' against possible invasion from France, the Catholic arch-enemy. The varied motives of the Scottish Parliamentarians have been discussed elsewhere (see Lynch, 1992 and Colley, 1992); more relevant here is the Scottish Parliament's desire to invigorate and modernise Scotland's economy, a need that had been highlighted by the famines of the 1690s and the costly failure of the country's colonial venture in Darien on the Panamanian isthmus at the end of that decade.

The Union signalled an intensification of economic activity. It eased restrictions on Scottish trade with England and benefited drovers, who profited from England's increasing civilian and military meat requirements. Political union and the sense that Scotland lagged behind her neighbour economically inspired increased interest in the agricultural advances that had been gradually developing in Holland and England. Determination to banish the threat of famine and to increase agricultural exports also inspired official support for new farming methods.

The Scottish Parliament had been passing Acts since 1660 designed to promote better farming methods and in the 1690s made it easier for landowners to institute the changes in arable and pastoral farming being tried out further south. Two Acts of 1695 authorised landowners to arrange the consolidation of runrig and the division of common lands for private use. The enduring political power of Scotland's landowning classes was evident in this legislation. Like the feuing arrangements and stricter tenancy laws of the previous century, enclosure maximised the lairds' control over land and allowed them to respond quickly to any commercial opportunity that presented itself. These Acts saved lairds intent on consolidating or enclosing land from having to enter into personal conflicts with their tenants.

Grazing fields for fattening cattle before market were the first enclosures to be made in Scotland: local demand for meat inspired their creation in the country around Edinburgh and English demand led to their development in the southwest. The enclosure of mains farms (generally those closest to the landowner's dwelling) occurred next, transforming them into separate, progressively farmed units. The enclosure of tenants' holdings came later, in the 18th and early 19th centuries.

Before the 17th century enclosures had been made to keep animals out of cultivation areas rather than to contain them. The construction of the new enclosures differed according to local conditions. Some were surrounded by hedge-and-ditches, with hedges planted on the ditches' spoil. Hedges were not always welcomed by the tenantry, who believed they sheltered birds and animals that threatened cereal harvests. When fields were cleared, enclosing dykes were sometimes built from the shifted stones and topped with turf.

In 1684 Sir David Dunbar, of Baldoon in Galloway, inspired by the proximity of the growing English market, enclosed enough grassland to support 1,000 beasts all the year round. Local landowners, including the Earl of Galloway, Sir Godfrey

McCulloch and Sir William Maxwell all followed suit. The subsequent increase of enclosed pasturelands in Galloway caused the Levellers' Rising there in 1724. The protest was triggered after a run of bad harvests left tenants hopelessly in arrears. Modernising landlords took advantage of the situation to evict indebted peasants and enclose their emptied farmtouns and common lands for commercial pastures.

The Rising of 1724 was the first recorded instance in Scotland of organised rural protest against the changes imposed by the commercialisation of farming. There had previously been a strong tradition of religious dissent in the southwest, where one protest had lasted for six months, led by a man described as a 'mountain preacher'. But the Levellers had economic motives: they pulled down dykes surrounding the new enclosures and demanded justice for the poor and the return of their newly-enclosed holdings. The most notable event occurred when a sizeable body of armed men attacked Baldoon's enclosure, pulling down its boundaries and killing 53 cattle they found there. Some of the activists were imprisoned but no one was executed as the authorities were keen not to provoke a wave of protest in the countryside. One of the Rising's results may have been to discourage lairds from making further Improvements in the southwest; opinion there was widespread dismay at the violence shown on both sides of the conflict but the episode certainly did not discredit Improvement objectives in the rest of the country.

After the famines of the 1690s there was a growing national sense that change was needed: Improvers talked, in the Enlightenment jargon of the times, of the need to 'rationalise' Scotland's farming. Rational equated with profitable for cash-hungry lairds: they needed money to join the affluent English pioneers of conspicuous consumption and to provide the dowries required to secure their daughters' success in the marriage market. Propagandists promised that Improvement would finance these aspirations by trebling farming profits.

Moreover, Enlightenment thinkers offered moral and cultural justification for landowners to improve their properties. Among Sir Francis Bacon's intellectual heirs, François Voltaire, David Hume and Adam Smith argued that natural science was a legitimate method of increasing human power over nature and that it was the duty of the state and the individual to use scientific knowledge for the advance of humanity. Manipulation and exploitation of the natural environment was, therefore, desirable: Improvement was a rational and ethical as well as a profitable duty. At the start of the 18th century, innovators like Lord Belhaven and John Cockburn of Ormiston adopted Improvement as a mission undertaken for the good of Scotland and her people. Others followed their example, employing a variety of new techniques to create efficient, integrated farming. Inevitably such changes had environmental impacts.

The legal right of Scottish landowners to prepare their properties for commercial farming by enclosure and division of common lands had been in place since the end of the 17th century. With their lands consolidated, Improvers were able to employ the new techniques and altering Scotland's damp, sterile soils was an essential first step. Collaborative effort to drain land had been authorised by Acts of Parliament in the 17th century but it was only ever applied once, to some peatbogs near Inchaffray on the River Earn. In the 18th century drainage became a priority on properties throughout the lowlands. Drainage, central to this project, increased fertility in rush-infested, boggy regions in the Lowlands where gley and peat dominated.

Enclosures were drained by open ditches dug around them and Improvers also tackled bogs, lochans and wet land generally, cutting and maintaining covered drains and ditches to remove water from both arable and pasture lands. The adoption of tiled drains in the 19th century made more effective underground drainage possible, facilitating the introduction of deeper, subsoil ploughing and the formation of flat fields. The human effort required for these drainage projects was immense. Fenton (1999) gives the remarkable example of one Ayrshire drainer, Thomas Wilson, cutting 9,140m of drains in a single year.

Drained environments also brought the benefit of a decrease in the feverish malarial chills caused by damp living conditions, as the *First Statistical Account* instances in the pre-Improvement

Perthshire parish of Abernyte: 'if a farmer in the spring wanted four of his cottagers for any piece of work, he generally ordered six, knowing the probability that some of them, before the work could be finished would be rendered unfit for labour by an attack of the ague.' The extensive draining of bogs and wetlands led to widespread and permanent habitat loss. There were complaints in the 1790s, for example, that draining the land had reduced lapwing numbers in Auchtermuchty. Plant species were also affected by loss of habitat.

In addition to draining, Improvers also applied lime to Scotland's acidic soils to improve fertility. Limestone was heated to produce calcium hydroxide, which neutralises acidic soil. In parts of southern Scotland where limestone and coal for heating it were readily available, liming had been practised since the 17th century. In 1604, Pont described fertile arable fields in Ayrshire as 'much enriched by the industrious inhabitants liming their grounds.' Skene of Hallyards suggested liming the infield before the cultivation of peas and in the 1690s, the writings of Lord Belhaven and Sir Robert Sibbald both stressed the value of lime, the latter with the warning that its misuse would pollute streams and be responsible for 'wasting the strength of the ground'.

To maintain productive soils, Improvers continued to utilise the dung produced by their herds but they also started to follow rotations of oats, peas and barley, regularly leaving some fields fallow. New crops featured in these systems: clover and ryegrass, which improved the fertility of fallow ground and provided enhanced grazing; and turnips and potatoes, which had hitherto been reared only as exotic oddities in lairds' gardens. Turnips kept the fallow ground clear of weeds and provided winter fodder. Sheds for storing turnips were built on Improved farms and new machines were designed to cultivate turnips in drills.

The potato evolved in the thin soils of South America's mountainous regions. The Spanish conquistadors discovered it in the 1530s, bringing it home to Spain in 1570. The Spanish did not prize their discovery: in their colonies the potato came to be identified as food for the poor and in Spain it was used to feed hospital inmates. The tuber did not reach the rest of Europe until after 1600 and remained a faintly sinister peculiarity until Improvers started to use it in both uplands and lowlands for the reclamation of rough ground.

Thanks to the new fodder crops, Scottish farmers could now feed their animals all year round, meaning that for the first time there was the possibility of fresh rather than salted meat in the winter months. Selective breeding of cattle had been taking place in Scotland since Neolithic times, and by the dawn of Improvement auroch and Celtic Shorthorn stock had lost their prehistoric ferocity and mobility after centuries of domestication. But the new capacity to overwinter beasts enabled more productive selection, which boosted milk and meat yields and literally changed the shape of cows.

In the late 18th century, to satisfy the growing demand for fine beef, traditional cattle strains from Angus and Buchan were crossed and recrossed to produce the Aberdeen Angus. Modern Highland Cattle were developed from traditional animals that gave the breed its wild spirit.

The Improvers introduced a range of new tools, initially copying mechanical grinders and winnowers from Dutch designs. By the 1780s Improvers throughout Scotland had begun to use lighter ploughs, such as the adaptation of the Rotherham swing-plough made by James Small, son of a Berwickshire farmer. These needed less manpower to operate; horses, which could be kept and worked more cheaply, often replaced oxen in pulling teams. Static and mobile mechanical threshing mills came into use throughout the Lowlands.

Before mechanisation of the harvesting process in the 19th century, Improved farms, shorn of the traditional communal workforce, had to employ seasonal migrant workers, most often Highlanders until the 1830s when Irish workers began to dominate seasonal employment on Scottish farms.

Although Improvement ideas were influencing farming in Holland, England and Scotland by the mid 18th century, Europe was still largely medieval. Not all Improvers' schemes paid off. Mistakes were made and experiments failed. New crops did not always prosper while trees planted round new enclosures spoiled yields with their shade. John Cockburn of Ormiston was not the only Improver to go bankrupt. During the first half of the 18th century only a minority of landowners opted for Improvement; the rest remained very conservatise.

There were compelling arguments against the cost and disruption of change. The absence of transport networks restricted opportunities to market farming produce. Wages continued to be paid at least partly in kind and lairds, especially in the north, remained reluctant to lose prestige by dispensing with their tenantry. In the Highlands and Islands, this tendency persisted beyond 1745. Crucially, there was insufficient justification for change when the system generally succeeded in feeding the population.

12

Lowlands Transformation

(1700–1800)

The old clumsy wooden plough became a thing of the past,
iron ones were substituted with machinery 'of a' dimensions,
shapes and metals' for clearing and pulverising the soil; draining
and fencing went on with an energy truly surprising.
(Samuel Robinson, *Reminiscences of Wigtownshire*, 1872)

THE LAST GENERAL FAMINES to afflict Scotland occurred between 1782 and 1784. This failure of agriculture to feed the country's population showed how limited the modernisation of the country's farming methods had been and made the country powerless to meet its food requirements in prolonged bad weather. In the 1770s as much as two-thirds of farmland in the relatively advanced regions of the Lothians, Angus and Dumfries-shire was still being worked traditionally.

Less than a century later, immense coal, iron, textile, chemical and engineering outputs made Scotland a global leader in manufacture and production, with the demands of the industrial workforce met. The enhanced yields were guaranteed by the deployment of farming practices that were admired and copied throughout the world. By 1851 the population of the country had more than doubled in a century, to nearly three million. Scotland in the 18th century was characterised by a mixture of socio-economic trends, some foretelling this stupendous development in human activity and some reflecting the enduring conservatism of traditional agricultural society.

The most significant of the modernising tendencies was the expansion of the cash economy. In the Lowlands after 1700, rents were paid increasingly in cash rather than kind and a growing part of the population there was receiving some wages in cash. A significant proportion of this ready money came from textile production.

Spinning wool to make yarn and weaving it into cloth had originally been part of domestic duties in Scotland's subsistence economy. Since the 17th century, however, Lowlanders had been using these techniques as part of the country's growing proto-industrialisation process. Spinning and weaving operations still took place in the home but woollen and linen products were now sold by the piece to merchants who paid for them in cash.

There is archaeological evidence that Bronze Age communities in Dundee cultivated linseed which can be processed to make flax fibre for weaving into linen. Linseed, brought to Scotland by Neolithic incomers, was first cultivated in the Fertile Crescent. Norse influence may have been responsible for the reintroduction of linseed cultivation to Scotland; medieval peasant farmers in the Lowlands grew linseed and hemp on heavily manured infield rigs to use in making their own cloth and ropes.

In the 16th century peasants on the shores of the Firth of Clyde and in southern Perthshire began to specialise in linen production, selling their finished products for cash. These payments represented a major departure from traditional subsistence agriculture and they produced rising standards of living in linen-making areas.

By the 17th century, linen, in the form of tablecloths, shirts, underwear, bags and ropes was being sent all over Scotland and to England. As demand grew, merchants began to supply the cottage industrialists with raw flax imported from Holland and the Baltic. Linen production was boosted in 1686 when the Scottish Parliament decreed that for lawful burial corpses must be wrapped in linen; by the 1730s it had taken over from wool as the country's most important textile.

The cultural influence of the Union and the benefits of free trade with England stimulated the linen industry's quality and style immensely, helping it to become one of Scotland's most successful 18th century industries. From London, the Board of Trustees for Manufactures and Fisheries urged Scots to grow more of their own flax; it also gave export subsidies to Scottish linen producers and arranged overseas trade for them.

Although linen manufacture went through peaks and troughs, overall production increased sixfold between the 1720s and the 1770s; at first only women and children were involved but when yarn spinning was mechanised, men operated the water-powered frames. The enhanced productivity earned record amounts of cash for the linen producers, although this bonanza did not come free of cost: the damp, stuffy atmosphere of domestic linen workshops proved a perfect breeding ground for tuberculosis infection. But such hazards did not undermine the rage for Improvement and the profits it promised. After the 1760s landowners increasingly promoted whatever cash-raising activities their properties would support: farming and mining as well as manufacturing.

Population Growth

The 1760s saw the start of sustained growth in the size of Scotland's population. The 1801 Census showed an increase of more than 300, 000 over the Reverend Alexander Webster's 1755 total of 1,265,380. This demographic trend may have been stimulated by improving climatic conditions as the 1690s saw the end of the worst effects of the Little Ice Age. But a human factor also contributed to this population growth: an improvement in Lowlands living standards which rose from the middle of the century until its end. Domestic textile production had been expanding since 1700 and meant ready money was available to the Lowlands population as never before. Later, non-food production diversified, mechanised and expanded in scale and brought increasing amounts of cash into Lowland peasant homes.

Significantly, population growth was rising faster in areas

where the new non-subsistence activities were being undertaken. Many members of the growing urban communities at East Kilbride, Glasgow and Deanston, for example, worked in textile production and the same link between population increase and the new enterprises existed in rural areas too. Between 1755 and 1801, the Lowland shires with the highest rates of population growth were those where coal and cotton production was rising like Lanark, Renfrew and Ayr. This population increase in the Lowlands caused unprecedented environmental impacts.

Of most immediate significance was the rise in demand for food caused by this increase in human numbers. Hundreds of thousands of new mouths to feed meant that grain prices rose sufficiently to convince Lowlands farmers that it was worth undertaking comprehensive reform of their farming methods. Now Improvements began to be made, not just at the whim of enthusiastic landowners but by conscientious tenants who could not afford to fail by defaulting on their rental payments.

Agricultural Revolution

By the 1850s farmtoun and rig had disappeared completely from the Lowlands to be replaced by the landscape of commercial agriculture with its compact, independent single-tenant farms, surrounded by enclosed fields and divided common lands. The peak in enclosing activity occurred between 1760 and 1815 in what deserves to be called an agricultural revolution. The emergence of a capitalistic market in agricultural produce triggered widespread uptake of Improved farming techniques. Tenants were also encouraged to make improvements by the longer leases authorised by the Entail Act of 1777. The impact of the changes in upland areas is demonstrated by the boast made by one Angus farmer in 1793 that 'The best crop of barley... in this parish is now in the stook on the summit of Dunnichen, 750 feet above the level of the sea'.

Soon no trace was left of the farmtoun landscape: Improving landlords simply removed the old dwellings, often consigning them straight to the midden. Alexander Fenton (1999) acknowledges the power of this transformation: 'the general effect... was to give Lowland Scotland a facelift that was probably more thorough than in any other country of Europe in the course of the 17th and 18th centuries.'

This heyday of Improving activity saw a frenzy of building in the Lowlands. Improved farms required entirely new structures for housing humans and animals and for the operation of modern agricultural processes. The new buildings were all made from stone although turf and straw were used as roofing materials until the advent of tiles.

The different elements of the new farms were built in the same order throughout the Lowlands. First, a solid, south-facing, stone farmhouse, followed by byres, stables and barns, lighter and airier than the structures they replaced. Barns were positioned and designed so that prevailing winds could assist the drying and threshing of cereals.

Last on the agenda were dwellings for farm labourers. The *Second Statistical Account*, compiled between 1834 and 1835, describes 'wretched pig-sty like huts... replaced by neat houses, with slated rooves, divided into two apartments.' In the more backward regions of the 'progressive counties' like Colinton and Heriot in Midlothian, workers' cottages were not built until the 1840s and 1850s. Workers' accommodation usually completed one side of a square formed with the other new buildings and with the dunghill in its centre. This arrangement evolved to reflect the social distance between farmer and labourers: trees were planted isolating the farmhouse from farm buildings, workers' accommodation and the dunghill.

As well as modernised farms, the transformed Lowlands also contained planned villages built by landowners as sites for new profit-making enterprises and to house the reduced workforce of the Improved landscape. The tidy geometrical design of these purpose-built settlements contrasted greatly with the huddled clusters of old farmtouns. The new villages accommodated the workers required to service the new farms, such as blacksmiths, builders, shoemakers, candlemakers and traders, and as the spread of proto-industrial activity undermined the monopolies of the burghs' specialist craftsmen, they also became centres for expanding craft production. Improvers were optimistic about their chances of establishing a prosperous, forward-looking countryside: about 150 planned villages were built in Scotland in the 18th century, the majority dating from between 1760 and 1815. Two examples are Bowmore on Islay, built in 1768 by the local Campbell laird to replace an older settlement; and Newcastleton, established in 1793 by the Duke of Buccleuch. A village's name sometimes signifies that it was originally planned: the word 'new' is a sure indication, as in New Lanark and New Pitsligo while personal names were often given to planned villages, for instance Port Charlotte on Islay and Jemimaville and Arabella on the Black Isle.

13

Industrialisation

...a people naturally possessed but of few territorial resources and living in a bleak and unpropitious climate, employing their activity, their constancy, and their genius to triumphing over a sterile soil... and making agriculture, manufacture and commerce, instruction, morality and liberty flourish together.

(Sir John Sinclair, *Analysis of the Statistical Account*, 1826)

THE RISE IN POPULATION NUMBERS between 1760 and 1780 triggered the vast project of rural reorganisation and boosted the country's industrialisation. The sharpest growth occurred in new or reinvigorated urban settings. Between 1755 and 1801, for example, Glasgow's population rose from 27,451 to 77,385 and Paisley's from 6,799 to 31,179. The wage-earning urban populations stimulated demand for manufactured products as well as the labour pool for mushrooming enterprises. Between the 1740s and the 1770s, industrialisation got under way in the Central Lowlands and started to cause impacts on the environment far greater in scale and intensity than any previously created through human agency.

The conversion of subsistence-related activity to proto-industrial wage-earning dominated this initial phase of industrialisation. Until the 1790s, when steam began to be used to power industrial processes, textile production was mostly carried out in the workers' homes. The sticky nature of flax fibres meant linen production could not be mechanised easily. Cotton yarn suffered no such disadvantages; it was produced from cotton wool imported from the West Indies. The new machines for spinning cotton yarn increased productivity by as much as 30 times by 1770.

Scotland's first cotton mill was set up at Rothesay in 1779. Entrepreneur David Dale, with Richard Arkwright, pioneer of mechanised spinning, as his business partner, opened their impressive new cotton factory complex at New Lanark in 1786. Its spinning machines used the power of water from the nearby Falls of Clyde, piped to the factory in a tunnel. Four years later William Kelly, the manager at New Lanark, connected the spinning machines to the steam powered engines invented by James Watt. Originally from Greenock and trained as an instrument-maker, Watt added a steam condenser to Thomas Newcomen's primitive steam engine making it more powerful and more fuel-efficient. Watt's engines were used all over the world, first as pumps but later as sources of power for manufacturing. Now that industrial machinery no longer depended on flowing water, large factories could be built in towns, making employment for those displaced farmtoun families that had gravitated to growing urban centres. By 1793 New Lanark housed the largest cotton mills in Britain and employed over 1,000 people. It was the site of the most substantial industrial enterprise in Scotland at that time.

The new urbanites worked entirely for cash wages; with neither time nor resources to undertake the old peasant crafts, they spent their wages (kept to what industrial entrepreneurs considered a desirable minimum) on wheaten panbread, cotton fabrics, metal-ware and other cheap products of the new manufacturing processes. The relative ease of the Lowlands' transition from subsistence agriculture to industrial production has been explained by the rise in labour living standards. Indeed, this industrially powered economic boom with its demographic roots in the 1760s lasted almost uninterruptedly in most Lowland communities there until the economic dislocations caused by the end of the Napoleonic Wars in 1815.

The enhanced efficiency of the new factories caused the price of cotton yarn to drop sharply. Demand for the cheap new fabric grew so quickly that cotton swiftly replaced linen as the most important textile industry in Scotland. Steam-powered cotton mills (and flax mills, until their decline in the 1850s) multiplied across the Central Lowlands from the last decade of the 18th century. The steam engines powering these new factories were all fuelled by Scottish coal.

Scottish coal had been used throughout the 18th century in the manufacture of glass, vitriol (the alchemical name for sulphuric acid) and iron as well as in the production of salt and lime, prompting a five-fold increase in coal output. Between 1750 and 1800 mining is thought to have employed the third largest group of workers in Scotland after farming and textile production.

In the Carboniferous Period tropical vegetation in the Midland Valley decayed into thick layers of peat. Over time these layers were buried and compressed into Scotland's main coal reserves; these were concentrated in a belt about 30 miles wide, running southwest from the Forth estuary to Ayrshire. Monks at Kelso and Newbattle had undertaken opencast coal mining to fuel their domestic heating and also their salt-pans. After the Reformation broke up the monastic estates, individual proprietors took over mining operations. They sold coal to commercial salt panners on the shores of the Firth of Forth and to the inhabitants of Edinburgh and Leith for domestic heating.

In the 17th century pit owners, including Lord Grange and the Duke of Hamilton, maintained highly repressive employment conditions designed to prevent colliers from seeking better pay and easier conditions in the more prosperous coalfields of Durham and Northumberland. Entire families could be legally bound to the service of a mine owner, whose rights over an escaped miner endured for eight years. Conditions in Scotland's eastern mines were particularly harsh.

As coal output was stepped up during the 18th century, many Scottish mines were enlarged and deepened, the only innovation made in coal extraction methods being the limited use of steam engines to pump water out of mines and lift coal to the surface. To attract an adequate labour force, mine owners gradually relinquished their tyrannical control of the workforce. Coal continued to power the country's industrial economy in the 19th century; when coal reserves in the Lanarkshire and Ayrshire coalfields started to run out, the expanding coalfields of Fife and Lothian provided alternative supplies. Lead mining was also undertaken in Scotland; records of lead mining at Leadhills and Wanlockhead, high in the Lowther Hills between Annandale and Nithsdale, go back to Roman times. In response to rising demand, the mines were enlarged in the 18th century and output levels continued to grow into the first half of the 19th century.

The Growth of an Industrial Infrastructure

Another important set of environmental impacts was caused by the development of Scotland's transport infrastructure. After 1700 well-heeled Edinburgh society became increasingly devoted to luxury and sophistication. The city did not decline after the loss of the Parliament but used the wealth and power acquired from its London connections to set the fashionable tone for the rest of the country. Water was piped in from Comiston, newspapers became available and clubs and taverns flourished.

In 1702 stagecoaches began to carry passengers between Edinburgh and Leith. John Home, Scotland's first skilled coachmaker, set up works in Edinburgh in 1738 and in 1749 a stagecoach service between Edinburgh and Glasgow started, the journey taking 12 hours. Inspired by the promise of increased business activity and rising land values, Lowland lairds began to commission the building of new roads. Before the end of the century, the compulsory labour service supposed to maintain the region's roads had generally been replaced by a more business-like system organised by committees of local gentry and financed by the proceeds from new toll-gates and turnpikes. Where it was efficiently instituted, the new system greatly improved existing road provision.

Ayrshire, having limited scope for transport by river, was one of the earliest counties to establish an effective turnpike trust. Landowners funded the parliamentary procedures necessary for building eight miles of road between industrial Kilmarnock and the port of Irvine. Acting as members of the county authorities, the gentry also enforced construction and maintenance standards on roads built by the county's committees. Ayrshire's example was followed throughout the Central Lowlands, with roads built linking settlements, canals and harbours to factories, coal mines, quarries, ironworks and dyeworks.

These networks benefited individual travellers as well as businesses. Improved industrial techniques helped to increase comfort and reduce journey times so that by the end of the 18th century the time taken to journey by coach from Edinburgh to Glasgow had halved. But topography and terrain, to say nothing of climate, continued to test Scottish travellers until the development of the railways after the 1830s.

Hilly terrain restricted the geographical spread of canal transport in Scotland, but as in England the expanding canal system was playing a major part in the development of industry and commerce. The task of deacidifying soil was using vast quantities of lime and of coal for heating it: canals could deliver these bulk cargoes efficiently. The Forth and Clyde Canal and the Monklands Canal were both completed in 1790. The Forth and Clyde Canal, connecting the two estuaries and the North Sea to the Atlantic Ocean, was envisaged as a symbol of national achievement but its organisation and financing proved arduous and protracted.

First contemplated in the 1740s, digging the canal from east to west finally began in 1768, with a workforce composed largely of Irish and Highland men wielding picks, shovels and wheelbarrows. Work progressed intermittently as finances continued to prove difficult. The completed canal, running 35 miles from the new port of Grangemouth on the Forth to Bowling on the Clyde, rose through 39 locks to a height of 156 feet; barges carried grain and flour to the west and coal and machinery to the east. The Monklands Canal took coal 10 miles into Glasgow. The Crinan, Union and Caledonian Canals were built in the next century but their economic value was limited and soon eclipsed by the railways. Until then, however, canals made the greatest human modification of the Scottish landscape since the Roman walls.

A major environmental impact of even more lasting practical importance was the deepening of the River Clyde. James Watt was designer and original engineer on the project which was begun in 1759 and continued in stages until its completion in 1809, when the estuary could start admitting ocean-going vessels.

By the 19th century commercialised farming, industrialisation and related infrastructures had made their marks throughout the Lowlands. Scotland's industrial products found ready markets at home and in England until the end of the Napoleonic Wars and even the financial turbulence of 1815 could not reverse the impetus of economic development in Scotland. Output rose and industrial progress continued (between slumps), reaching new levels of production and profit in the next 100 years. As well as alterations to the landscape caused by the economic transformation of the region, industrialisation also caused unprecedented pollution.

The Start of Industrial Pollution

We came na' here to view your warks
In hopes to be mair wise
But only, lest we gang to hell
It may be nae surprise.
(Robert Burns, outside the gates of the Carron
Iron Works, 1787)

From the middle of the 18th century, iron foundries, workshops, breweries and distilleries all proliferated to meet the demands of the new wage-earning consumers. This initial, water-powered phase of industrialisation affected the country's streams, rivers and lochs. Discharges into these waters from mills, factories, distilleries and mines were joined by the sewage and other effluent generated by urban settlements. Sewage produced toxic effects on the environment as well as threatening public health in towns. Industrial pollution had even more devastating environmental consequences. Solids like sawdust and washings from coal and lead mines could destroy entire river ecosystems by reducing oxygen levels, smothering plant and animal life and damaging spawning beds. Distilleries produced acid waste and woollen mills discharged alkaline soap and wool washings.

The development of textile mills led to the disappearance of salmon in the Gala and Teviot rivers, while coal washings from the Ayrshire pits were blamed for destruction of fish in the River Nith. By the end of the 19th century, salmon and trout had disappeared from most rivers in the industrialised parts of the western Midland Valley. Near lead mines, high mortality rates occurred among children employed to wash the mined ore.

Large bodies of water were equally vulnerable to industrial contamination. Since medieval times the shores of the Firth of Forth had been the site of coal mining, salt manufacture and other industrial processes. In 1527 Boece informed his readers of the rich marine fauna to be found there, including cockles, oysters, saithe, pollock, 'merswine' (porpoise or dolphin) and whales; he ends his list with 'quhit [white] fische'. The disappearance of this cornucopia was the result of urban waste disposal as well as industrial pollution.

Two large-scale enterprises were established early in the region's industrialisation which produced new levels of pollution. Dr John Roebuck, a Yorkshire-born entrepreneur-inventor, was in at the start of both.

Vitriol was used extensively in the new textile, soap and metal-manufacture industries. In 1749, Prestonpans Vitriol Manufactory was set up. Medieval monks had pioneered salt production at Prestonpans and from the 16th century salt was used for various industrial processes including the manufacture of pottery glazes. This local tradition of technical skill, the proximity of the coalfields and the market guaranteed by nearby East Lothian bleachfields, helped the Prestonpans Vitriol Manufactory to become the biggest in Britain by the 1780s. Pollution from corrosive sulphuric acid fumes was extensive near the Works and acid deposition affected adjacent soil, water and vegetation as well as damaging human and animal health.

Ten years later, Roebuck was involved in establishing the

Carron Iron Works, on the Carron River near Falkirk. Using iron ore from Bo'ness and coal from Kinnaird, the Carron plant with its extensive range of water-powered furnaces, forges and mills was constructed on an enormous scale compared with earlier rural smelting furnaces like the one set up at Bonawe near Taynuilt, Argyllshire in 1730. The Carron Works was Scotland's first large-scale industrial production unit; its debut triumph was the manufacture of cannonballs, foreshadowing the firm's achievements in arms manufacture during the 19th century.

The Works' coal- and coke-fired smelting furnaces produced substantial and unprecedented effects on their immediate environments. One Sunday in 1787, Robert Burns arrived to sightsee. After being refused admission, he registered the protest against the Works' visual impact which introduces this section.

The universal adoption of steam powered a second stage in Scotland's industrialisation, which was in full swing by the 1830s. Coal burning caused pollution beyond its immediate locale, releasing volumes of chemicals into the atmosphere, notably nitrogen oxides and sulphur dioxide. These compounds react with water, producing nitric and sulphuric acids, and fall as acid rain; in the absence of moisture, they are deposited on the environment as dry dust.

This acid pollution had significant effects on Scotland's environment. Acid rain sped up the weathering of stone buildings while the acidification of lochs and rivers caused disease in fish. Acid deposition on soils disrupted plant and tree growth, with thin upland soils particularly vulnerable to such damage.

Many of the small-scale 18th century industries had caused localised acid deposition. Sulphurous fallout from volcanic eruptions in Iceland also produced acid deposition in Scotland. However, evidence from sediments in Scottish lochs shows that around 1800 more substantial and constant acid deposition began to take place. Blown on the wind, this acidic pollution came from the coal-burning factories of northern England as well as those of the Scottish Lowlands. Over the next century this pollution intensified as growing populations burnt more coal for domestic heating and to power expanding industrial production.

Vitriol was used in a bleaching method which involved boiling, rinsing and soaking fabrics in a mix of acids and alkalis (sour milk, lye and urine had been used before vitriol) then laying them out to dry, exposed to sunlight. Contemporary prints show woven fabric drying, crop-like, in enclosed fields. The entire labour-intensive process, carried out mainly by women, took three months for cotton and six for linen.

Its highly corrosive nature led to the replacement of vitriol as the Scottish textile industry's preferred bleach before the end of the 18th century. Responsible for its eclipse was Charles Tennant (1768–1838). Born in Ochiltree, Tennant's life coincided with the first hectic phase of industrialisation. He started work as an apprentice weaver, became a bleacher at Darnley near Barrhead, and in 1799 patented a bleaching agent using chlorine and slaked lime (calcium hydroxide), which became a worldwide commercial success. It revolutionised bleaching by doing away with the endless steeping and boiling and reducing the required exposure to sunlight from months to days. Tennant's St Rollux works in Glasgow was the largest chemical works in the world in its 19th century heyday. The manufacture of Tennant's bleach powder created pollution by releasing hydrogen chloride into the atmosphere, where it became highly corrosive hydrochloric acid. There was no use for hydrogen chloride and at first factory owners saw no reason to prevent its escape, but the result was an immense deterioration in air quality near chemical works, the destruction of plant life and the corrosion of buildings and iron railings. A chimney over 100 metres high was built at St Rollux for the purpose of diffusing released gases. Tennant's Stalk, as it became known, did not dispose of the pollution but only channelled it away from the factory site.

Chemical pollution aroused public complaint throughout industrial Britain and in 1863 the first Alkali Act authorised the Board of Trade to establish an inspectorate for monitoring 'noxious vapours'. The legislation may have had only limited effect but it was the beginning of state regulation of industrial pollution. The purity of air and water was now officially recognised as an important political issue.

14

The End of Subsistence Agriculture

1782–1784: Scotland's Last Grain Famine

There never was such a Generall scarcity of Provender...
(William Forbes, grieve of Castle Grant, Strathspey, March 1783)

IN THE LOWLANDS after 1760 new farms were laid out and factory towns grew. In overcrowded and unsanitary Edinburgh, developers drained the Nor' Loch in preparation for the replacement of the capital's tottering tenements and stinking wynds. Plans were drawn up for 100 acres of elegant sandstone houses interspersed with squares and gardens and laid out in spacious grids; they would be completed by 1800 to form the New Town. But despite these modernising tendencies, much of the Lowlands remained unchanged. Nearly a quarter of a century after these progressive trends began, a reminder of old afflictions was visited on the entire country as populations again experienced dreadful vulnerability to famine. From the icy spring of 1782 to the long, bitter winter of 1783–84, starvation stalked uplands and lowlands alike. This would be the last time consecutive years of harvest failure caused famine throughout the entire country. Never again would subsistence crises more serious than localised, short-term grain shortages occur in the Lowlands. After the 1780s, Improved farming and effective transport networks in the southern half of the country were increasingly able to counter bad weather and poor soil: new canals and roads were used to take grain and lime to communities where harvests had failed or soil fertility was inadequate.

But at the start of the 1780s, the threat of famine was not yet banished from the Lowlands, agricultural Improvement had not been universally implemented and the construction of roads and canals was only just beginning. Moreover, the first half of the decade saw some of the harshest climatic conditions in Scotland since the Little Ice Age. From the spring of 1782 until harvest-time in 1784 the weather proved disastrous for communities throughout the land.

The 'Black Aughty-Twa' earned its name from the first manifestations of this catastrophic climatic episode. In the spring of 1782 wintry conditions were slow to pass and they returned so soon in the following autumn that snow fell on unripened crops. In October, the gloomy report came from the north that 'The crop at Wick, Caithness, afforded a most melancholy spectacle, being while quite green, covered with frost and snow at the beginning of the month.' In many places grain could not be harvested until Christmas by which time it was only fit for animal fodder.

The following July the Laki volcano in Iceland underwent a massive eruption. Over one quarter of Iceland's population perished in what was remembered there as 'The Year of Famine'. Laki erupted intermittently until the following February, releasing a fog of sulphate aerosols which covered western Europe, causing thousands of deaths from respiratory disease. In Caithness 1783 was known as 'The Year of the Ashie': crops and pastures were covered in tephra, sulphurous volcanic fallout.

Sulphate particles in the atmosphere made 1783 and 1784 especially cold throughout Scotland and snow spoiled harvests in uplands and lowlands alike. In the summer of 1784 the Lowlands were still experiencing food shortages: in June Edinburgh's Canonmills Distillery was attacked by a mob angered at the diversion of grains and vegetables from human consumption to liquor production. However, in these two years of suffering and shortages, famine was avoided by northern communities where potato cultivation had been adopted. Agricultural Improvers first introduced the potato to the Highlands in the 1770s. It tolerated the acidic soil and low temperatures, but its adoption was not universal and starvation took a dreadful toll amongst populations reliant on oatmeal. Life in the northern uplands was still particularly hard and vulnerable to any deterioration in growing conditions. The advantage conferred by the potato in the famine years confirmed the general sense that farming in the Highlands would benefit from Improvement. Production could be commercialised, waste land reclaimed and enriched, and linen manufacture and fishing could swell rural wages. There seemed every reason to be optimistic and, apart from these very difficult years in the 1780s, the four decades following 1760 were ones of unprecedented economic activity in the Highlands.

1760–1800: False Dawn in the North

Keeping at work many hundreds of persons in divers kindes of manufactures; brought from beyond sea the skillfull'st artificers could be hired for money; to instruct the natives in all manner of honest trades... induced masters of husbandry to reside amongst my tenants, for teaching them the most profitable way of... hedging, dunging, sowing, harrowing, grubbing, reaping, threshing, killing, milling, baking, brewing [improvement] of pasture ground, mowing, feeding of herds, flocks, horse and cattel; making good use of the excresence of all these; improving their herbages, dayries, fruitages; setting up the most expedient agricolary instruments of wains, carts, slades with... wheels and axle-trees, plows and harrows of divers sorts... and all other manner of engines fit for easing the toyl and furthering the work...

(Sir Thomas Urquhart's vision of economic development in the Highlands, *Logopandecteision*, 1653)

Despite the years of climate-induced disasters, economic confidence continued to run high in the north in the second half of the 18th century. Landowners and politicians believed that the

region's traditional economy could be transformed, just like the
that of the Lowlands, into orderly profitability by the rational
application of Improvement principles. The former frequency of
armed cattle raids had thwarted plans for enclosing and enhancing
pastures and for selective cattle breeding; the region's lawlessness
had generally discouraged trade.

But Culloden's victors were able to dismantle the legal and
cultural foundations of the 'wild wikkid' tribalism that had
haunted Lowland imaginations for so long. In 1747 Highland
society was officially disarmed as the population (apart from
drovers) was forbidden to carry weapons. Bagpipes and traditional
Highland dress were outlawed and the legal powers of clan chiefs
were abolished. Many Jacobite leaders fled to France and a few
were executed in London.

This removal of some of the most traditionally-minded
magnates cleared the way for Improvement. The old order's
insistence on the military value of large retinues conflicted with
new strategies for streamlining agricultural production and
increasing yields. Since the start of the 18th century, interest in
modernisation had been growing throughout the north, among
Jacobite as well as loyalist landowners. Their traditional influence
was gradually being diluted. The sons of many Highland lairds
were no longer being fostered by favoured clan members in
the old style. Instead, increasing numbers were being sent
away to be looked after by the families of respectable Lowland
proprietors. The young lairds-in-waiting were shown the practice
and profitability of new land management techniques and new
industries; many returned north infected with Lowlands faith in
the necessity and desirability of Improvement.

The Westminster Government wanted innovation and
commerce to follow demilitarisation. After 1746 control of the
rebel chiefs' massive acreage (reaching north–south from Loch
Broom to Stirlingshire and east–west from Braemar to Glenelg)
was given to the Commissioners for Forfeited Estates. The
Commissioners, mainly drawn from the Edinburgh establishment,
were determined to replace what they saw as the Highlanders'
savagery and ignorance with the progress and respectability that

were taking hold in the Lowlands. The Commissioners planned to use the rents of the annexed estates for 'better civilising and improving the Highlands' and 'preventing disorders there for the future'. To these ends, the Commissioners promoted Improvement methods in the north.

They began by undertaking a detailed survey of the lands under their control and went on to instruct tenants on the forfeited estates about commercial farming techniques – enclosure, crop rotation, drainage and the use of winter fodder. Many of the Commissioners were also members of the Board of Trustees for Manufactures which was already supervising industrial developments in the Lowlands; for the Highlands, the Commissioners planned new model villages on Lowland lines. One such was Beauly, an Inverness-shire town on the frontier between the mountainous hinterland and the eastern coastal plain. Here the Commissioners hoped sober industry could be made to replace the tendencies of the native population whom their agent considered to include 'many perverse and obstinate fellows of bad character'. Landowners in the same spirit of Improvement and commercial enterprise also built or refurbished villages, including Oban, Grantown-on-Spey and Tomintoul.

Fishing had long contributed to human livelihoods throughout Scotland, especially in places like the northwest and the islands where farming potential was limited and marine resources especially rich. Many late 18th century landowners and Government officials believed sea and river fishing would play a central part in the hoped for economic transformation of the Highlands and Islands.

Herring had been Scotland's most important catch since medieval times, when it supplied domestic and overseas markets. It was caught in nets from small open boats close to the shores of both Forth and Clyde estuaries. Fishing was also important in Orkney and Shetland, where it supplemented subsistence farming. Orcadians used boats for inshore line fishing and pursuing whales when they appeared. The Shetland Islands' fishing grounds were superior to those of the Orkneys; the Dutch controlled the herring fishery there until 1700. The trade was then taken over by

Shetland landlords who forced their tenants to take employment in the herring fishery and pass its profits on as rent.

Western sea-lochs such as Torridon teemed with herring: Shieldaig, the name of the settlement at the head of the loch, means herring bay in Norse. But in the late 18th century commercial fishing hardly existed on the northern mainland west of Moray. Settlements and sheltered landing-places along Highland coasts lacked the necessary infrastructure of harbours, piers and storehouses. Improvers believed that fishing could offer employment to those made redundant by new farming methods, in the same way that manufacturing was providing work for former farming populations in the Lowlands. For the Duke of Sutherland's tenants evicted to the coast, fishing was a difficult necessity.

The Westminster Government supported the proposed fisheries with serious cash investment as part of its Improvement agenda for the north. It was also motivated by the naval threat from France and by hopes of exploiting herring resources rather than leaving them to the Dutch. The Government also wanted a new marine infrastructure to advance the general state of British transport and an active fishery to provide naval recruits.

Plans were drawn up in the 1780s for a chain of fishing villages, with facilities for landing and curing herring, to be established on the Highland coast from Dornoch on the east coast to Arran on the west. The British Fisheries Society, whose membership overlapped with the Board of Trustees for Manufactures and with the Commissioners for the Forfeited Estates, eventually scaled down these ambitious proposals. For the south and north of the Minch respectively, Tobermory (formerly called Ledaig) and Ullapool were chosen as the main foci of the Society's schemes. Tobermory, completed in 1788, had a fine natural harbour and housing for the fisherfolk.

For three decades, from 1788, Thomas Telford was employed by the Government to develop the Highland infrastructure. In 1801 this remarkable man (the stonemason son of a Dumfries-shire shepherd who became President of the Institute of Civil Engineers) undertook a survey of Highland roads and bridges. Between 1804 and 1824, he supervised the construction of

900 miles of road and 120 bridges in the north. Telford also oversaw the design and construction of the Caledonian Canal between 1803 and 1822. All told, he was responsible for an unprecedented impact on the Highland environment, which he and his Government employers believed would foster trade and prosperity there.

Telford's first project in the Highlands was undertaken for the Fisheries Society. In 1788 he designed and built the brand new village of Ullapool on 1,500 acres of the Wester Ross coast. The development, with stone piers, barrelling houses and a salt store, cost the Society £10,000 (Telford worked for a reduced fee). Such was official confidence in the likely volume of trade at the new port that a customs house was erected on Isle Martin in Loch Broom. Accommodation was also constructed for the ex-servicemen that the Society hoped would settle in the new village and labour at the fishery while their wives and children were employed in linen manufacture. Settlers were also encouraged to come and work at the fishing in the coastal villages of Shieldaig and Plockton in Wester Ross. Private landlords tried to establish fishing communities on the west coast: the Duke of Argyll at Oban and Macleod of Macleod at Dunvegan on Skye.

In 1790 the Society employed Telford to survey existing harbours and piers in the north; following his recommendations, facilities were built at east coast ports including Poultneytown at Wick. At around this time, the Society also re-organised the herring trade on more productive lines: to improve quality it introduced extra payments called bounties for properly cured fish and these were increased in 1809. Around the turn of the century landowners were intensifying the exploitation of salmon stocks by establishing rivermouth netting stations.

As early as the 1750s many landowners in the north had been taking a variety of practical steps to exploit their lands more effectively. On the sheltered, fertile lands of the Cromarty Firth, Sir Thomas Urquhart's dream of economic development in the Highlands seemed to be coming true.

Sir Robert Munro of Foulis, before his death fighting on the Hanoverian side at the Battle of Falkirk in 1746, made extensive plantations on his estates below Ben Wyvis. His son, Harry, returned from the fighting to rebuild Foulis Castle, which had been attacked by rebels. Sir Robert's grandson, Hugh, inherited in the 1780s and embarked on a thorough implementation of the new farming methods. His farm manager grew the first commercial carrot crop in the north. By the 1830s, sawmills and grain mills had been built on the Foulis estate, land had been reclaimed from the sea and local agriculture was considered to be in a very advanced state.

For the first time since the climatic deterioration of the Bronze Age, tree cover expanded in the northern uplands. In the Lowlands, Improvers were planting and harvesting trees and their Highland counterparts followed suit. Their plantations changed the northern landscape in the century following Culloden. Trees were grown to shelter exposed farmlands and to sell as timber.

Oak bark was used in tanning, charcoal for smelting and deal planks for the numerous buildings that Improvers erected in these years. Improving Highland proprietors cashed in on the export of these raw materials. The Foulis estate, for example, sold its own timber and planted more trees, including oak, beech and Scots Pine, then known as 'Scotch Fir'.

Another member of the clan, Sir Hector Munro of Novar, spent the proceeds of his Indian army career on the spectacular development of his estate. He planted its bare hillsides with millions of trees, including the first larch ever grown in the district. Further inland, Sir Hector Mackenzie of Gairloch built a handsome modern house by the side of the Conon river. The *First Statistical Account* applauded his innovations:

> this place has of late been much Improved by art. There are plantations of firs on this estate of considerable extent. Some of them are intermixed with forest trees, and all of them in a thriving condition. Where dismal bleakness lately prevailed, the eye is now presented with refreshing verdure.

Highlanders were receiving cash payments for an increasingly valuable range of exports, traditional and new. Cattle-droving, one of Scotland's most important preindustrial ventures, had been significantly boosted by the Act of Union in 1707. Since that date, the British Army and Navy had served in numerous European conflicts including the War of the Spanish Succession (1702–14), the War of the Austrian Succession (1740–48), the Seven Years War (1756–63) and the American Revolutionary War (1776–83). The wars against post-revolutionary France began in 1793 and continued, on and off, for over 20 years. These extensive military deployments meant consistent demand for meat to feed the troops; it was supplied by the drovers' Highland cattle, fattened in the Lowlands and England. By the 1780s, cattle prices had reached record levels and would remain high until the peace of 1815. During this time, hundreds of thousands of beasts were driven from all over the Highlands and Islands to be bought by Lowland and English dealers at lowland trysts.

Another important cash earner for the Highland population during these years was the export of whisky. In the 17th century ale made from bere or barley had been the favoured drink of the Highland peasantry. Production of aqua vitae for more occasional private consumption was undertaken in many better off households and the possession of domestic stills for this purpose was widespread. As the century drew to a close the products of this cottage industry started to be taken south, sometimes by drovers, to be sold for cash.

Possession of a domestic still was legal; selling the spirit it produced was not. However, not all Highland distillers operated illegally. The Forbes family of Culloden owned a distillery at Ferrintosh on the Black Isle. In 1690 Duncan Forbes was instrumental in defusing a Jacobite plot; he was compensated by the Westminster Government by an exemption from excise duties in exchange for a single annual toll of 400 merks, regardless of the volume of whisky his stills produced. Ferrintosh became synonymous with high quality whisky and local woods were cleared for its production. Even when the exemption was withdrawn in the 1780s, whisky production continued to flourish there. But many, many other Highland distilling operations existed that were not legal, especially after 1707 when the Act of

Union subjected them to English taxation. This meant all whisky producers had to pay significant duties or operate illegally. Many landowners turned a blind eye to illicit distilling by their tenants and some accepted whisky as rent.

By the 1730s the drink was becoming known by the Gaelic name for aqua vitae: *uisga-beatha*. It was smuggled to the Lowlands and to England by Highlanders taking the chance to convert often indifferent barley into valuable merchandise free of Government tax. Their remote and inaccessible bases helped them evade the Excise men and their duty-free spirit undercut the legal trade. Before 1823, when excise regulations changed, there were possibly as many as 20 illicit stills in the Highlands for every legal one.

The whisky trade was given a further boost in 1736 when London's moral panic about increasing gin consumption inspired the Gin Act which increased the duty on Madam Geneva. Whisky consumption rose accordingly, swelling both legal and illegal whisky profits. A quarter of a century of war against France helped the trade still further as whisky was drunk instead of French claret for patriotism's sake.

Kelp manufacture was also bringing cash profits to the north. Today kelp is the collective term for the large brown seaweeds, like tangle (laminaria digitata), and cuvie (laminaria hyperborea) which grow on rocky parts of Scotland's coastline. Coastal populations had been using seaweed to fertilise their soils since prehistoric times. Martin Martin (1703) mentions the benefits to island crops of being 'manured by sea-ware'.

In the 18th century kelp referred to the ash formed when the large brown seaweeds were burnt. The ash, an alkaline substance, was used in the manufacture of soap, glass and textiles. The Westminster Government protected the kelp industry by imposing high import duties on barilla, a cheaper alkali produced in Spain. The Napoleonic Wars stopped all trade with Europe, further boosting the value of home kelp production.

Populations on the Hebrides, the Orkneys, and parts of the northwest mainland were employed in the laborious manufacture of kelp. In the summer months, men cut the seaweed and brought it onto the beach. After it had been left to dry on stone dykes, women burned the seaweed in long pits lined with stones, using hay and heather to keep the fire going for up to eight hours. Next, men used iron mallets to pound the ashes into a solid substance, which was then covered with stones and turf and left to harden. Approximately 24 tonnes of seaweed produced one tonne of kelp, which was broken into lumps before being shipped off to ports in southern Scotland and England.

James Miller's splendid history of the Pentland Firth (1994) includes a contemporary account of how Orcadians detested the smelly discharges produced by kelp manufacture. The islanders

> were certain that the suffocating smoke… would sicken or kill every species of fish on the coast or drive them into the ocean far beyond the reach of the fisherman; blast the corn and the grass on their farms; introduce diseases of various kinds and smite with barrenness their sheep, horses and cattle and even their own families.

The profits from the kelp industry accrued by landlords hiking up rents are illustrated by Ranald George Macdonald, 18th Chief of Clanranald, who held land from Arisaig to Moidart on the mainland and the islands of South Uist and Benbecula. Rental income was no more than £1,000 per annum before the beginning of kelp manufacture, rising to nearly 20 times that amount at the peak of the kelp boom. Clanranald was not alone amongst Highland proprietors in his taste for conspicuous consumption. He spent fortunes on luxurious living in London, ploughing none of his kelp profits back into his properties.

The Failure of Improvement in the Highlands and Islands

It was clear by 1800 that the Highlands and Islands were not responding to the Improvement schemes that had been transforming the Lowlands since 1760. A large proportion of the Highlands and Islands' population was still engaged in traditional agriculture and the absence of manufacturing activity in the region that Burt had noted in the 1730s was virtually unchanged.

George Dempster, a wealthy Dundonian, was determined to reverse this position. In the 1780s, he bought Skibo estate on the shores of the Dornoch Firth. An Edinburgh advocate, Dempster moved among the top ranks of Enlightenment intellectuals; he was also a business associate of David Dale in his cotton manufacturing enterprises at New Lanark and Stanley. In 1793, Dempster invited Dale to build a large cotton mill at Skibo. At its busiest, the mill, in its new hamlet of Spinningdale, employed over 100 workers to operate Dale's spinning machines. But the business was too distant from suppliers and customers, and did not prosper. When fire destroyed the mill in 1808, it was not rebuilt and no significant Highland manufacturing project followed in its wake. Investment in Highland industrial development was deterred by the region's remoteness and its lack of coal, the new power source for manufacturing in the Lowlands.

Human factors were also responsible for the failure of Improvement plans in the north. Improvement ideology clashed with the conservatism of Highland society which was too firmly entrenched to have disappeared with the defeat of the Jacobites. Many landowners held a lasting belief in the importance of the size of a laird's retinue. This accounted for their acquiescence in the years after Culloden when tenant numbers grew and holdings had to be subdivided into ever tinier portions to accommodate new families.

This population increase in the north was due in large part to potato cultivation. The adoption of potatoes as a staple crop became universal there after the grain famines of the 1780s: by 1800, potatoes were providing up to four-fifths of Highland food requirements. The potato thrived in lazybed cultivation and, unlike oats and barley, could withstand heavy rainfall and high winds. Moreover, potatoes were harvested in August, two or three months before oats or barley and they also provided vastly superior yields to those of grain crops: one boll of potatoes planted produced up to 20 bolls harvested compared to seven bolls harvested from one boll of grain planted. As pressure on land increased, such considerations were vital.

Most landlords did little to discourage dependence on potatoes and some (including Clanranald) actively promoted it because the new crop sustained growing numbers of rent-payers. The resulting fragmentation of landholding structures ruled out the consolidation of land essential for Improvement strategies. Many of the tenants were as reluctant to change as their lairds. Kelp and whisky manufacture, droving and potato cultivation were all activities which did not threaten old communal values. Traditional loyalties could be easily exploited by unscrupulous landowners forcing tenants, for the sake of clan ideals, to accept deepening poverty. The Gaelic language, still despised, feared and incomprehensible in the Lowlands, limited the Highlanders' options and made it harder for them to think of moving south.

While economic development transformed much of the rest of Britain, environmental factors continued to dictate the history of the Highlands and Islands. The obstacles they presented to Improvement is illustrated by the Annexed Estates Commission's survey of a typical northwest Highlands property, the Barrisdale Estate in Lochaber.

Barrisdale had no flat arable land. Oats, the only crop which could be grown there, needed intensive manuring with seaweed or bracken. The Commissioners' report listed other difficulties with cereal cultivation on the estate: 'the tediousness and expense of delving [the steep fields had to be dug with a spade, like most upland arable in the Highlands and Islands], the frequent and heavy falls of rain in the spring, summer and autumn, the danger and uncertainty of reaping, and the steepness of the hills.' The report describes one Barrisdale farm which had 'a most horrid appearance from the steepness of the hill and the numberless impending rocks... which bring on great losses to the tenants by the death of their cattle occasioned by falls from the rocks when in search of their food.' On this sort of land, the Commissioners had to conclude, there was no potential for new farming methods apart from enclosing land to grow hay crops: the region's infertility could not be altered as the expense of bringing lime north was prohibitive. Highland difficulties could still be intensified by bad weather: although the worst of the Little Ice Age was over after the 1780s cold spikes continued to occur, wrecking harvests and causing localised famines in the uplands. Outside the kelping districts, the tenantry, inured to the privations of subsistence farming on thin, exposed soils, were generally so poor that Improving landlords had little hope of raising rents to swell their own incomes.

Plans for the herring fisheries were only partly realised. The closing decades of the 18th century were in fact the last when herring shoals were plentiful on the west coast. As a proponent of the western herring fisheries had to acknowledge, 'The herring be indeed a whimsical as well as a migrating animal.' After 1800, the herrings transferred to the east coast where from Caithness to Aberdeen open-boat inshore herring fishing flourished for half a century. This boom led to the successful development of east coast ports, including Fraserburgh and also Peterhead where, as well as fish, seals and whales were landed and processed. Dundee also became a major whaling port. But the story was different on the west coast where herrings never proved plentiful enough to sustain the scale of fishery originally envisaged as an engine of economic development.

After herring deserted the western sea-lochs, larger boats were required to reach more distant stocks. Insufficient numbers of ex-servicemen came forward to work in the new industry and the British Fisheries Society was unable to find tenants for its new houses in Ullapool. Many of the villages established as fishing centres became more dependent on farming than fishing. Some, like Oban, many metamorphosed into tourist destinations as the 19th century progressed.

The failure of the western fisheries to support a string of bustling coastal villages producing fish and linen was symbolised in the 19th and early 20th centuries by the extensive employment of women and girls from northern communities as itinerant herring gutters. With few employment opportunities at home, the 'Scotch fisher girls' followed the herring fleet as it tracked the migrating fish. They travelled down the east coast as far south as Great Yarmouth, gutting and sorting the catch.

The importance of the region's migrant labour force reflected the general disappointment of northern Improvements hopes and its terrible implications for those staying put. By 1800 the proprietors' need for cash was forcing them to introduce a type of farming untried north of the Great Glen 40 years earlier, commercialised wool and meat production using Improved sheep breeds.

The first of these flocks to arrive was the Blackfaced Linton, joined later by the Cheviot. Based on the Borders' Long Hill sheep, the Cheviot was a mix of Merino, Ryelands and Lincolnshire stock. Highlanders called it *caoraich mhor*, the Great Sheep, and were astonished by its size and ability to survive northern winters unhoused. Landlords were most convinced by Improved Cheviot yields: the supremely sturdy beast produced a third more wool and meat than the original Cheviot breed.

By the 1780s the new flocks had been brought as far north as Ross-shire; in 1792 Sir John Sinclair had 500 breeding ewes installed on his Caithness property. He encouraged fellow proprietors to follow his example: 'The Highlands of Scotland may sell at present, perhaps from £200,000 to £300,000 worth of lean cattle per autumn. The same ground will produce twice as much mutton and there is wool into the bargain.'

The need to boost revenue was becoming urgent. A generation of more polished landowners was taking charge in the Highlands. Many saw themselves as belonging to the fashionable echelons of the British establishment and paid costly visits to Edinburgh and London. Their rental incomes still included payments of potatoes and whisky and set amounts of harvest work and peat cutting. The most valuable slice of traditional farming wealth was the tenants' black cattle, sold to drovers for cash to pay the rent. The price of these animals peaked in the 1780s. Its sharp decline after 1815 left landowners, especially those without kelp, eager to modernise their properties in order to charge higher cash rents. Failure to increase revenue might mean having to let lands or even sell them outright.

Indeed, as cattle prices fell, landowners' debts mounted and more and more did have to sell up. Their widespread replacement by incoming proprietors began the final demolition of traditional social structures in the Highlands.

In the new century, a large body of tenants was no longer something for a landowner to be proud of unless there was a cash crop to be gathered in. The new sheep farms offered cash dividends to the landowner while guaranteeing the tenantry nothing but conflict and ruin. The logic of bringing sheep to the Highlands became more and more irresistible and would-be proprietors queued up to invest in Highland pastures.

As has been widely recounted, commercial sheep farming proved disastrous for the existing tenantry and was the final blow to the old cattle economy. From the 1760s existing settlements, their lazybeds and grazings were emptied (sometimes forcibly) of their human and animal inhabitants and replaced by sheepwalks, as the new sheep pastures were termed. Grazings, including the fertile shielings, were reserved for the imported sheep.

Tenants were left with nowhere for their stock. Sheep farmers detested the Highlanders' goats and brown fine-haired brown sheep for their threat of cross-breeding and infection. Goats tended to escape: feral and domestic numbers grew so vast that in one year, at the end of the 17th century, 100,000 Highland goat and kid skins were sold in London. But for Improvers, traditional flocks, rife with parasites and prone to scab, symbolised farming's unprofitable past.

Sheep farmers did not tolerate the black cattle either. In 1791, two Cameron brothers from Lochaber leased land for a sheep farm from Sir Hector Munro of Novar. The property was at Kildermorie, west of Strathrusdale, in the hills above the Cromarty Firth. Some former tenants retained rights to graze cattle on high ground bordering the new farm. Conflict broke out in the following year. Their cattle strayed into the sheepwalk, where the Lowland shepherds employed by the Camerons swiftly impounded them, and the dispute turned violent when the tenants repossessed their beasts. The incident triggered a region-wide protest against the new sheep farms, which signalled disruption and misery for traditional communities. Demands were made for lower rents and increased provision of arable land for the tenantry.

Plans were drawn up to drive the new flocks out of the county. The scheme began when protesters visited the properties of Sir John Lockhart Ross of Balnagowan, a shady incomer with Borders sheep farming connections. Sir John had set up Ross-shire's first sheep farms; some of the tenants they displaced, who had tried unsuccessfully to resist eviction, were among the protesters in 1792 as they gathered all the Balnagowan flocks from Strathoykel, Glen Achany and Strathcarron. Soon the drove reached Kildermorie, ready to collect the Camerons' beasts and proceed south. But alarmed local gentry, unsettled by upheavals in revolutionary France, called the Black Watch from its barracks at Fort George to defend the rights of private property. The leaders of the Ross-shire Insurrection, as the press excitedly dubbed the incident, melted away into the hills before the soldiers could catch them. The crimes committed by the drovers were reminiscent of 'wild wikkid' conflict-resolution, still alive in popular Highland memory. The men were eventually apprehended and tried; their light punishments indicated general sympathy for victims of the new farming regime.

The lesson of Kildermorie was not lost on modernisers. In future, all communities being 'removed', as the Improvers euphemistically termed the clearance process, must be completely banished from the new sheep pastures. Kildermorie proved the impracticability of allowing remnants of the old ways to linger on the margins of the new.

Over the next 100 years the conflict between tradition and commerce was played out, inflicting varying levels of pain and distress on traditional tenants. They were powerless to avert change. From the 1770s the price of wool rose and landlords responded accordingly. In 1811 there were approximately 15,000 sheep in Sutherland; by 1855 there were 205,000. Similar increases occurred in Ross-shire, Argyll and Inverness-shire in the same period. After the coming of the sheep, land throughout the Highlands and Islands was increasingly under the control of outsiders. Parvenu proprietors and traditional landowners alike now tended to employ professional lowland factors to carry out Improved farming methods on their properties.

Patrick Sellar, a native of Moray, trained as a lawyer in Edinburgh, and another Morayman, William Young, worked as factors for the Duke of Sutherland. Between 1807 and 1816 they carried out the clearance of tenant communities in Kildonan, Strathnaver, Assynt, Lairg and Farr to make way for sheep farming enterprises. Sellar was responsible for some of the most callous demolitions of human settlements carried out in the Highlands for this purpose.

The Reverend Donald Sage, Minister at Achness, watched his parishioners' suffering as Strathnaver was cleared. To the dispossessed:

> the dark hour of trial came in right earnest. It was in the month of April, 1819 that they were all, men, women and children, from the heights of Farr to the mouth of the Naver, on one day to quit their tenements and go – many of them knew not whither, for a few some miserable patches of ground along the shore were doled as lots without anything in the shape of the poorest hut to shelter them. They were supposed to cultivate the ground and occupy themselves as fishermen. Many had never set foot in a boat.

The misery of these mass evictions was seen again and again throughout the north after 1800, exposing the failure of lowland Improvement methods to bring general prosperity. The sheep farming regime did not offer tenants any chance of employment. Herding these newfangled flocks was unfamiliar to Highlanders; the work was performed by south-country shepherds used to the new breeds. As James Hunter (1999) points out, the skills, bravery and hardships of these shepherds are generally omitted from Clearance narratives.

The self-contained sheep farms did not become hubs of economic growth. Indeed, apart from the success of east coast fisheries at ports like Wick and Helmsdale, few new economic projects did succeed in the Highlands and Islands. Unlike the Lowlands, the north did not see developments that provided jobs for those dispossessed by agricultural modernisation. Concerned onlookers saw through the Improvers' public promises of universal prosperity. As a local minister wrote in 1818 to James Loch, another of the Duke of Sutherland's factors:

> From what I know of the circumstances of the majority of those around me since so many were sent down from the heights to clear Sellar's farm, I do not perceive how the great addition, which is intended to be made to their number can live comfortably as you anticipate.

The End of Traditional Farming Society in the Highlands

It was a sorrowful peace for me for it cost me £4,000.
George Williamson, Aberdeenshire cattle dealer, on hearing the bells of Perth ringing to celebrate the end of the war against Napoleon)

In 1815 the end of Britain's global conflict with France caused a severe economic downturn throughout Europe. The same year, a colossal volcanic eruption at Tambora on the Indonesian island of Sumbawa spewed sulphurous clouds into the upper atmosphere. Consequent cold weather caused widespread harvest failure in 1816, exacerbating post-war problems. Suffering in the Highlands and Islands started the last, painful act in the demise of traditional farming life.

Droving profits slumped with the peacetime decline in Britain's military beef requirements, while the practice of raising huge cattle herds to be sent away for sale was rendered obsolete by winter fodder and the selective breeding of cattle. New, heavier breeds were unsuitable for the long tramp to southern markets. In the end, farmers preferred the speed and efficiency of mechanised transport for their livestock. In the 1820s cattle fattened in the Highlands and Islands and the northeast were taken to market in the holds of steamships. A cattleman quoted by William McCumbie in *Cattle and Cattle Breeders* (1867) gave an idea of the animals' conditions on board:

I went down to the hold among them but I was glad to get back with my life, and although you had given me the ship and all aboard her, I would not have gone back.

With fewer cattle to move, drovers now took flocks south from the new sheep farms. However, after 1848 railheads at Perth and Aberdeen undermined the trade further. Droves continued to be made to the Falkirk Tryst until the end of the century but by 1860 new provincial auction houses established at Perth, Oban and Inverness became the main foci of the northern livestock trade.

Barilla imports resumed after 1815, halving kelp prices. In the 1820s the Leblanc process for alkali manufacture was adopted in Glasgow. This made the industrial use of kelp obsolete and prices fell further. Nevertheless, in some of the poorest Highland communities kelp manufacture continued until the middle of the 1830s by which time kelp was fetching only £2 per ton.

The export of illicitly distilled whisky proved as vulnerable to outside forces as that of cattle and kelp. In 1823, the Westminster Government's Excise Act removed the economic advantage of illicit distilling and within a decade, the value of contraband Highland whisky exports had been wiped out. Cottars who relied on whisky production to pay their rents were cleared from the land, especially where landowners wanted to install Improving tenants. The minister of Birse, on Deeside, noted that 'considerable number of families formerly supported by illicit distillation have been obliged to remove to town and other parishes'. The Duke of Sutherland opened a licensed distillery in Clynelish near Brora and evicted scores of tenants from nearby Lairg and Rogart whose livelihood had depended on contraband whisky.

The general decline in cash-earning enterprises caused rents to collapse and many Highland landowners had to sell or let some or all of their lands. Some decamped to southern suburbia. Their successors joined in presiding over the end of traditional Highland society.

A new wave of investment in sheep farming provoked more clearances, lasting until the 1860s. Rents for land required for sheep farming hiked up rents beyond tenants' capacity to pay. Evicted for non-payment or simply cleared, tenants were resettled on inferior marginal ground. Landlords justified this by arguing that tenants would now have time for other cash-earning occupations. It was in these inauspicious circumstances that the crofter emerged, with a cash-oriented identity and a foreign name, distorting echoes of traditional subsistence farming. Populations in the southeast Highlands were able to seek alternative employment in nearby manufacturing districts but suffering was extreme in the rest of the region. Hardest hit were the remotest areas with least opportunity of non-agricultural employment: on the northern mainland and in the Western and Northern Isles crofters had to take seasonal employment away from home in east coast herring fisheries and on Lowlands farms. Increasingly, people thought of emigrating.

Peace worsened Highland problems but it did free would-be emigrants from the charge of shirking their patriotic responsibilities. As despair over the lack of opportunities intensified, people started to leave the Highlands in growing numbers, bound for the industrial cities of lowland Scotland and England and to colonial and other overseas destinations. Mass emigration, under way since the 1760s, was a logical reaction to uncertain conditions at home.

Among the early emigrants were independent, moderately well resourced tacksmen who could see that their position in clan society would not survive the changes which were starting to affect Highland life. Some chartered their own ships and took their followers to recreate traditional clan society in Canada and north America. One such was John Macdonald of Glenalladale, a Clanranald tacksman. He foresaw the impending crises and the suffering they were likely to entail for the clansmen 'unless some other path were struck out for them.' Accordingly, he purchased land on the island of St John, in the Gulf of St Lawrence off Canada's east coast and in 1772, led an expedition of tacksmen and tenants from Arisaig, Moidart and South Uist to settle there. It was later estimated that this early, voluntary phase of emigration saw as many 20,000 people leave the Highlands for good.

George Dempster vehemently opposed emigration as the

solution for the Highlands' problems. He (and others, including Sir John Sinclair) believed, like Sir Thomas Urquhart, that the successful exploitation of Highland resources could make the region prosperous without destroying existing communities. Dempster did not make his Sutherland lands over to sheepwalks but instead granted Improving leases to his tenants. Dempster believed that reorganisation and investment could overcome obstacles to Highland Improvement. Other proprietors, however, had more selfish reasons for halting emigration.

Landlords' ancient reluctance to reduce tenant numbers turned to greed for kelping profits. In 1803, the Highland Society, representing landed proprietors, used spurious safety concerns to lobby for legislation against the trade in shipping emigrants away from the Highlands and Islands. Fares were raised beyond tenants' means and emigration slowed down until 1815. Thereafter, worsening economic conditions led to calls for increased opportunities to emigrate. Poverty and hopelessness intensified.

The end of the kelp industry also spurred emigration from Orkney. There too, population increase and congestion occurred at the end of the 18th century. Fishing and whaling and the Canadian fur trade provided non-agricultural employment for islanders but shrinking landholdings kept up emigration rates into the 19th century. After 1850, peasant farming largely gave way to cattle-rearing for a healthy export trade using the new steamship routes from Orkney to Aberdeen and Leith.

In 1827 the legislation of 1803 restricting emigration from Scotland was repealed. More and more landlords were now keen to empty their communally occupied lands and rent them profitably. Historically, 'deer forests' meant pieces of land that night or might not be wooded, but where game was protected for the king's sport. After 1603 these lands were sold off piecemeal by the Crown to private landlords. In the late 18th century the advent of sheep farming in the north inspired landowners to sell off or let deer forests to sheep farmers with the result that perhaps no more than ten remained in Ross-shire and Sutherland in 1800. After 1815 sporting tenants started leasing land in the Highlands and Islands. The chance of deer stalking, grouse shooting and salmon fishing attracted sportsmen from all over Britain and beyond. Hunting and fishing opportunities in England and southern Scotland had been reduced by industrial degradation of rural environments. In the 1830s the price of wool started to drop. Sheep farming became a less attractive proposition and more lands were let or sold for sport. By the end of the decade 28 new deer forests had been established in the north, some on former sheepwalks. Sheepwalks in Glenstrathfarrar, for example, were turned over to deer in 1827, as was the Kildermorie sheep farm in the 1840s.

Sporting estates in the Highlands and Islands represented the climax of the process which brought the wild, autonomous lands of the north and their peoples under the economic and political control of the London-based ruling elite via its representatives. Military penetration and subjugation of the region had been followed by its use for amenity. Queen Victoria bought property on Deeside in the 1840s and the British plutocracy hurried to follow her lead. The spread of sporting estates in the north was inspired by the example of the royal consort, Albert, an enthusiastic if ineffectual deerstalker. Continuing rail expansion breached the Cairngorms and the Monaliadh to reach Inverness in 1863; by 1874 lines from there to the north and west coasts gave visiting sportsmen access to some of the north's wildest areas. The trend to convert land for sport intensified after the 1860s and by the end of the century sporting estates covered over 2.5 million Scottish acres.

There were several cold spikes in the decades following 1815 with localised famines and outbreaks of potato blight causing subsistence crises throughout the north. Potato blight, a fungal infection, reduced entire crops to inedible slime overnight. Harvest failures in 1827 forced the people of Barra to the beaches in search of cockles. The local minister was sure that without the shellfish, 'there would have been hundreds dead this day in Barra.' Scenes of this sort were repeated throughout potato-dependent regions until the dreadful outbreak of 1846 (and beyond until the blight-free years that followed 1857).

An especially virulent strain of blight was carried from America in a cargo of potatoes landed at Ostende in 1845. Insects, wind and rain spread the infestation which reached Ireland before the year's end. Entire regions in Ireland had become completely dependent on the potato crop: possibly more than a million people died of hunger there in that year. The following year, westerly winds blew blight spores to Scotland. Once a symbol of Improvement, the potato had in fact prolonged subsistence farming. In the grain famine of the 1780s, potatoes had saved their cultivators from starvation. In 1846 dependence on potatoes caused appalling suffering for entire communities.

To make matters worse for upland populations, 1846 saw a marked drop in global temperatures following the atmospheric effects of the eruption of Fonualei, a volcano in the South Pacific. The tenantry's distress in the face of these harsh conditions, provoked a mixed response from landlords. Some supplied their tenants with oatmeal to substitute for the ruined potato crop. Many more, however, made no provision for their starving tenantry.

John Gordon, an Aberdeenshire landowner, was one of Scotland's wealthiest men. By 1840 he had acquired the old Clanranald lands of South Uist and Benbecula and bought Barra and Eriskay from another bankrupt laird, McNeill of Barra. Gordon earned notoriety for the inhumane treatment of his Hebridean tenants. Government reports on the effects of potato blight singled out his properties as displaying the worst 'wretchedness and privation' witnessed in the north: crofters on Eriskay shared out plots of grass and herbs between themselves. On Barra dysentery, cholera and typhoid broke out; diseases became prevalent throughout the north in these famine years.

Rent arrears were increasingly used as a pretext for eviction and to justify the view that Highland properties could not be made to support an extensive tenantry and that the best solution for overpopulated communities was emigration. Some 19th century landlords were so keen to empty their Highland properties that they subsidised their tenants' departure. In 1826, for example, MacLean of Coll, the landlord of Rum, paid for the population of that island to be shipped to Canada. This cost was amply covered by the rent MacLean subsequently received from letting Rum to sheep-farming tenants. Even relatively benevolent landlords like James Matheson on Lewis and the Duke of Argyll on Tiree were ultimately compelled to encourage their tenants to emigrate. Others, like John Gordon, used force and guile to compel their tenants to leave.

By the 1840s traditional tenants could see clearly that sporting estates, like sheep farming, would mean their own exclusion and dispossession. Sporting interests clashed painfully with those of crofters. Gamekeepers protected deer populations for the benefit of the shooting tenants. Deer caused dreadful damage to growing crops and sportsmen also caused havoc in the crofters' fields, as a witness from Skye told the Napier Commission of Inquiry into the Conditions of Crofters and Cottars in 1883: 'The English sportsmen would be shooting in our corn. The women who would be quietly herding would have to fly home for fear of bullets.' The declining droving trade was further undermined by sporting estates whose owners refused access to drovers and their herds.

These enforced curbs on traditional livelihoods and the absence of other profitable employment signalled the end for many Highlanders, especially after the horrors of repeated potato blight. Emigration offered the only escape from hunger and despair. Official encouragement to emigrate took the shape of meagre financial assistance and entire communities departed on leaky boats. By the 1870s the northern half of the country had lost a large proportion of its human inhabitants. In 1755 the population of the Highlands and Islands was 51 per cent of the Scottish total; in 1881 it was 21 per cent. The human suffering implicit in these figures was not the only result of the changes in land use experienced in the Highlands and Islands after the 1760s. They also had serious implications for the non-human environment. These outcomes are, however, less clear-cut and scientific understanding of them is still at an early stage.

After the 1870s, the notion that commercial sheep farming had damaged northern environments gained wide acceptance and there was much talk of 'sheep-sick pastures'. In the previous decade, an outbreak of liver fluke in the English sheep population had boosted Scottish sheep prices and subsequent overstocking was later blamed for reduced fertility on northern hill-grazings. Pessimism about fertility levels might have also been linked to the downturn in demand for Highland mutton and wool caused by new refrigerated imports from Australia and New Zealand.

The invasion of the Highlands and Islands by millions of sheep did not cause the treeless state of much of the region. But the extreme changes in land use from traditional pastoral subsistence agriculture to commercial sheep farming (followed in many places by deer forests) did have environmental impacts. The total absence after the early 18th century of animal predators on sheep and deer allowed unprecedented numbers of those species to live unmolested in the Highlands and Islands. Such a huge population of grazing animals must have affected plant and animal species in the region.

Alexander Mather (Smout ed, 1993) has shown that between the end of the 19th century and 1975, a decline in the breeding fertility of sheep occurred in the Highlands and Islands, as indicated by declining lambing yields. Although such a decline suggests a deterioration in the nutritional value of hill-grazing, the exact causes are difficult to identify. Factors like climate trends, stock management, breeding techniques and the presence of deer might all be implicated in the declining fertility of the region's sheep pastures.

'Green lands' and 'black lands' developed where traditional farming had formerly been practised. 'Green lands' appeared on former cultivation sites and heather-covered 'black lands' formed on less fertile areas. The long-term effects of sheep and deer grazing reduced fertility on the 'green lands'. The end of traditional farming also meant reduction in the manuring of arable ground, and hill and other grazing. Muirburning and other regular clearing of vegetation intensified in some districts under the new regimes and ceased altogether in others.

The droving trade's cattle herds declined in size after 1815. These herds had trodden down bracken, which sheep flocks did not. Bracken growth had also been restricted by its traditional use as fertiliser and roofing material. The new farming regimes may, therefore, have promoted the spread of bracken in parts of the Highlands and Islands.

Increasing deer numbers added to the grazing pressures created by sheep farms. Such pressures can effect species distribution. For example, the presence on northern pastures of the invasive tufted hair grass (deschampsia caespilosa) may have been the result of overgrazing by sheep, although deer might have been partly responsible. Another possible result of the presence of massive sheep flocks in the Highlands is the increase in carrion-eating birds. Buzzards, kites and crows all benefited from increasing numbers of sheep and lamb carcasses. But the activities of gamekeepers and their sporting employers in this period also reduced these birds' numbers significantly.

The End of Preindustrial Society in Scotland

Traditional farming's eclipse in the Highlands and Islands began with the political and social changes that followed Culloden. Its final replacement by commercial sheep farming and the management of land for sport marked the end of preindustrial society in Scotland. By 1800 subsistence farming in the Lowlands had been swept away by the commercialisation of agriculture and the effects of industrialisation. Its eclipse in the Highlands and Islands began with the political and social changes that followed Culloden and was completed by the introduction of commercial sheep farming, the management of land for sport and crofting. By the 1860s, preindustrial society in Scotland was no more.

Long before c.1000 ce, postglacial climate change and human activity combined to reduce Scotland's vegetation and associated animal species, with upland regions most severely affected. The resulting poverty of the Highlands and Islands' environment relative to that of the Lowlands shaped much of Scotland's subsequent history. England's superior extent of fertile territory seriously disadvantaged her northern neighbour in the countries' preindustrial conflicts.

Environmental factors also dictated the course of industrialisation and modernisation and their different regional forms.
The Lowlands were transformed by new agricultural methods,
industrial growth and urbanisation; the Highlands and Islands,
although less physically altered, lost entire human communities
to radical economic change. Mass emigration emptied the region
where the landscape's austere beauty is sometimes mistaken for
unspoilt naturalness; as this account has shown, the reality is
more poignant and also far more complex.

The importance of environmental forces, especially climate, in
preindustrial history is plain. Scientific, industrial and agricultural
developments have strengthened humanity's powers to resist these
forces so effectively that their decisive influence on human life is
sometimes forgotten. The dominant role of environmental factors
in Scotland's history illustrates our ultimate dependency on non-
human forces, this understanding of the past equips us better to
understand, debate and meet the challenges of the future.

Chronology of Environmental Impacts on Scotland's Population

Understanding climates which predate the start of written records relies on the analysis of a range of sources including fossilised pollen, ice-cores, tree rings, glacier histories and sediments in bogs and lochs and on the seabed. Radiocarbon dating can help to identify the timing of weather events. All entries refer to Scotland unless otherwise specified. Apart from individual events such as storms and volcanic eruptions, all dates are approximate.

3 billion bp: Formation of coldest rocks in Scotland.

410 million bp: Scotland and England join.

400 million bp: Caledonian Orogeny.

60 million bp: Atlantic Ocean formed.

2.4 million bp: Beginning of the Quaternary.

30,000 bp: Start of last major glaciation.

18,000 bp: Wasting of ice cover begins.

11,000–10,000 bp: Loch Lomond Stadial.

14,000 bp: Earliest recorded human presence in Scotland.

10,000–9,000 bp: End of last glaciation, formation of soils, arrival of first plant and animal colonists. Climate warms and some postglacial moisture evaporates.

6000 bp: Climatic Optimum. Warming continues until tree lines stand over 300m higher than at present.

6000 bp: Land links between British Isles and the European mainland submerged. British Isles' climate now maritime.

6000 bp: Elm Decline.

3164 bp: Icelandic volcano Hekla erupts, depositing ash in Scottish peats.

4000/3000–500 bp: Climatic deterioration (probably triggered by Hekla eruption); weather much wetter and colder. Tree lines fall; upland settlements and cultivation abandoned.

200 bc–440 ce: Partial recovery from climatic deterioration with increasingly warm, dry summers. Some very cold winters occur but they cause few lasting environmental effects.

400–440 ce: Increased storminess.

440–800: Climate cooler and stormier.

600–700 ce: Climate cooler and wetter with storms and floods on North Sea Coasts. Abandonment of settlements in southwest Norway.

763–764 ce: Severe winter across Europe.

770–800: Colder winters, droughts and frosts. Start of Viking expansion, largely triggered by the poverty of their land resources, exacerbated by cold conditions in Denmark and Norway.

800–1300: Medieval Warm Period. More documentary evidence about climate available because of the development of feudal society, especially in the Lowlands. Climate warms throughout this period with upper limits of tree growth and cultivation over 300m above sea level. The retreat of polar ice and reduced storminess enables Viking expansion, including voyages to Iceland, Greenland and Canada.

859–60 ce: Severe winter across Europe.

900 ce–1100: Low rainfall, warm summers and cold winters.

1000 ce: From this point onwards natural change begins to be less influential on Scotland's non-human environment than the activities of the human population.

1100–1300: Few spring frosts and no widespread famines.

1209: Floods in Perth wash away its royal castle.

1100–1250: Feudal government established (initially by David I, who supports new burghs and monastic houses); European cathedral building represents peak of medieval culture.

1300: Kelso Abbey cultivates cereals at 300m above sea level and extensive vineyard expansion is planned in England.

1300–1400: Colder, wetter climate causes abandonment of upland farms and settlements. Vineyards fail in England.

1300–1850: The Little Ice Age. This period is characterised by episodes of predominantly low temperatures, with averages for the whole period being 1 degree Celsius lower than today's, and also by a relentless variability of seasonal climate.

1310–1550: Cooling and storminess prevail as climate undergoes sharp deterioration in the first decade of the 14th century. Evidence from peat bogs shows increased moisture in the Scottish environment throughout this period.

1315–21: Wet and cold spring and summer weather causes a series of harvest failures in Scotland and across Europe resulting in widespread, extreme famine.

1332–33: Floods in China kill millions of people and cause widespread habitat loss: rats carrying bubonic plague are displaced westwards.

1347: Bubonic plague in the Crimea.

1348: Bubonic plague arrives in England: the Black Death.

1349–50, 1361–62: Black Death in Scotland.

1362: Major volcanic eruption in Iceland.

1407–08, 1422–23: Severe winters in Scotland and northern Europe: the Baltic freezes.

1430s: Series of severe winters and harvest failures causes famine in Scotland and the rest of northern Europe. Wolves forced to seek food are active from Smolensk to England, their last reported presence in that part of Britain.

1500: Population rises throughout Europe for the first time since the 14th century.

1550–1700: Approximate climax of the Little Ice Age. Falling ocean temperatures cause increased storminess in the North Sea. Documentary evidence on climate expands with the establishment of the early modern state and the 17th century's scientific revolution.

1550–1600: Poor harvests are frequent in Scotland.

1600–20: Harvests recover.

1612: Plantation of Ulster by James VI/I and first general emigration from Scotland in the opening decades of the century; both are responses to frequent crop dearths and climatic difficulties.

1620s: Hard winters and late springs cause local crop dearths and widespread loss of livestock.

1630–60: Indifferent harvests combine with the effects of civil war to reduce grain supplies throughout Scotland.

1650: Instrumentally obtained climate records start to be made.

1670: Severe winter followed by poor harvest.

1674–75: Heavy spring snowdrifts cause loss of livestock and poor harvest.

1690–1720s: Permanent snow on Cairngorms and other mountain summits; polar ice floes spread southwards forcing Inuit kayaks south.

1694: Sandstorm obliterates farmlands to create Culbin Sands, Moray.

1695–1700: Low summer temperatures lead to bad harvests and extensive famine.

1697: Sandstorm obliterates the Udal, a sizeable village on North Uist.

1725–26: Severe winter followed by poor harvest.

1730–60: Climate starts gradual improvement as average temperatures rise; grain prices stabilise and few shortages are reported. Some climate variability persists throughout the 18th century.

1740s: Hard winters; the last of the Scottish wolf population shot.

1750s: Favourable weather in the second half of the century facilitates the successful adoption of agricultural innovations in Scotland.

1782–84: Scotland's last grain famine.

1783–84: 'The Year of the Ashie' in Caithness: volcanic dust from a major eruption in Iceland destroys crops in the north of Scotland and reduces temperatures throughout the country.

1815: Huge volcanic explosion at Tambora.

1816: 'The Year Without Summer' sees temperatures dropping throughout the northern hemisphere. Rain and frosts spoil harvests throughout Europe and food riots and epidemics follow. On Glasgow Green, a crowd of 40,000 protesters demand a reduction in bread prices.

1827: Potato famine in the Highlands and Islands.

1836: Potato famine in the Highlands and Islands.

1845: Potato famine throughout Ireland causes deaths estimated at over one million.

1846: The volcano Fonualei in the South Pacific erupts, causing global drop in temperatures.

1846: Potato blight throughout the Highlands and Islands.

1847–57: Localised potato blight intermittently affects Highlands and Islands.

Chronology of Human Events in Environmental History to 1845

*c.*14,000–13,000 bp: Evidence in Lanarkshire of Scotland's earliest human presence.

*c.*10,000–9000 bp: Formation of soils, arrival of first plant and animal colonists.

*c.*7000–6000 bp: Arrival of first farmers with livestock and crops.

*c.*5750 bp: First chambered tombs at Maes Howe, Orkney.

*c.*4500 bp: Bronze Age technology.

*c.*4000 bp: Callanish, Neolithic monument, Isle of Lewis, built.

*c.*3700 bp: Last stone circles built in Scotland at Clava, Inverness-shire.

*c.*2725–2500 bp: Iron Age technology

*c.*2500 bp: First crannogs built.

*c.*2320 bp: Earliest recorded eye-witness account of Scotland as Pytheas the Greek circumnavigates Britain.

*c.*2100–1900 bp: Northern brochs built.

All dates Christian Era from this point.

43: Romans invade and occupy England.

*c.*79: Romans land in northeast Scotland.

84: Battle of Mons Graupius.

118–124: Hadrian's Wall built.

140–150: Antonine Wall built.

*c.*250–500: Scots settle in Argyll.

297: First written reference to Pictish people.

367: Roman forces retreat from Scotland after an alliance is formed between the Picts and Scots.

*c.*450: First written reference to kingdom of Britons centred on Dumbarton.

565: Columba founds abbey on Iona.

795: Vikings attacks begin with raid on Iona.

*c.*800–850: Northern Isles colonised by Vikings.

834: Cinead mac Alpin crowned King of the Picts.

1124–1286: The Canmore feudalisation of Scotland.

1295–1328: Wars of Independence.

1385: First record of guns purchased by the Scottish monarchy.

1504: Ratification of Scottish Parliamentary Acts establishing feuing (passed 1458).

1560: Protestant Reformation in Scotland.

1603: Regal Union with England.

1695: Enclosure Acts.

1707: Act of Parliamentary Union with England.

1759: Carron Iron Works founded.

1760–1860: Highland Clearances.

1790: Steam first used in cotton manufacture.

1799–1815: Napoleonic Wars.

1815: First sporting tenants in the Highlands and Islands.

Scotland's Monarchs

This is like a Pictish king-list, a dynastic record more informed by blood lines than historical reality. Many of the early kings had their lives ended, directly or indirectly by their successors. Regents usually represented their own interests or those of noble factions rather than those of the Crown.

Kenneth mac Alpin 843–858

Donald I 858–862

Constantine I 862–877

Aed 877–878

Giric & Eochaird 878–889

Donald II 889–900

Constantine II 900–943

Malcolm I 943–954

Indulf 954–962

Dubh 962–966

Culen 966–971

Kenneth II 971–995

Constantine III 995–997

Kenneth III [+ Giric?] ?997–1005

Malcolm II 1005–34

Duncan 1034–40

Macbeth 1040–57

Lulach 1057–58

Malcolm III 1058–93

Donald III 1093–94

Duncan II 1094

Donald III (returned) 1094–97

Edgar 1097–1107

Alexander I 1107–24

David I 1124–53

Malcolm IV 1153–65

William I (The Lion) 1165–1214

Alexander II 1214–49

Alexander III 1249–86

Margaret 1286–90

Interregnum 1290–92

John Balliol 1292–96

Interregnum 1296–1306

Robert I 1306–29

David II 1329–71

Robert II 1371–90

Robert III 1390–1406

James I 1406–37

James II 1437–60

James III 1460–88

James IV 1488–1513

James V 1513–42

Mary 1542–67

James VI (and I) 1567–1625

Regal Union with England 1603

James I 1603–25

Charles I 1625–49

Charles II 1649–85

(1651–60 Cromwell's military occupation).

James VII 1685–89

James Francis Stewart, The Old Pretender, son of James VII
1688–1766

Charles Edward Stewart, the Young Pretender 1713–83

William III and Mary II 1689–1702

Anne 1702–14

Parliamentary Union with England 1707

The Shape of Scotland

843: Cinaed mac Alpin, as King of Alba, takes control of territory composed of Pictland and Scotland. Pictland consists of territory north of the Forth including Orkney, Shetland and the northern Hebrides; the territory of the Scots is based in Argyll and the southern Hebrides.

945: Control of Cumbria including Strathclyde ceded to Malcolm I by Edmund of England in return for defensive help against the Danes.

c.971–975: Edgar of England hands control of Lothian to Cinaed II for the same anti-Danish motives as in 945.

1018: Malcolm II defeats a Northumbrian army at the battle of Carham to confirm Scottish possession of lands between Forth and Tyne.

1059–93: Malcolm III fights with England for control of Cumbria, Westmoreland and Northumberland until he is killed in battle at Alnwick.

Duncan II (1094) and Edgar (1097–1107): feudal vassals of England.

David I (1124–53): attempting to achieve a border with England based on the Rivers Eden and the Tees, takes advantage of civil war in England to press for possession of Cumbria, Northumberland and Westmoreland; he secures Carlisle and Newcastle.

1157: Malcolm IV (1153–64), young and politically weak, loses momentum in struggle for Border territories, which Henry II reclaims.

1174: William the Lion (1165–1214) captured at Alnwick attempting to seize control of Border territories. Treaty of Falaise confirms Scotland's subordinate position to England.

1237: Alexander II signs Treaty of York renouncing Scottish claims to Cumbria and Northumberland. The Border is fixed at the Tweed–Solway line.

1296–1547: These years see intermittent civil wars in Scotland frequently involving English forces. These are often very destructive conflicts and make Scotland's southern borders extremely fluid. Control of Berwick and Roxburgh. for example, changes hands several times. In 1460, Scotland recaptures Roxburgh but in 1482, Berwick is lost to England. But the Border, unlike that between England and Wales, is never marked by fortifications. Its precise line continues to be the subject of conflict, dealt with by a special court for 'Debatable' areas. Drawing juries from both countries, the court sits intermittently until the 17th century.

1547: Battle of Pinkie, the last battle between the kingdoms of Scotland and England.

1560: Treaty of Berwick marks the beginning of the end of Scotland's historical conflicts with England. European developments make England keen to avoid further military engagement on her northern Border and Scotland's Protestant aristocracy are able to form an alliance with Tudor co-religionists against the threat of France. James VI grows up as a Protestant prince with his eyes set on the prize of the English succession: the Regal Union of 1603 marks his success and the end of armed conflict between the two countries.

1266: Treaty of Perth, Norway cedes the Western Isles to Scotland.

1468–69: Christian I of Denmark, Sweden and Norway pledges Orkney and then Shetland to Scotland as part of his daughter Margaret's dowry for her marriage to James III.

Bibliography

Applebaum, S (1958) Agriculture in Roman Britain, *Agricultural History Review*.

Armit, I (2003) *Towers in the North*, Tempus, Stroud.

Ash, M (1991) (eds Macaulay, J and Mackay, MA) *This Noble Harbour: A History of the Cromarty Firth*, John Donald, Edinburgh/Invergordon Port Authority.

Ashmore, PJ (1996) *Neolithic and Bronze Age Scotland*, Historic Scotland/ Batsford, London.

Bacon, F (1999) *New Atlantis*, in (ed. Bruce Susan) *Three Early Modern Utopias* Oxford University Press.

Barclay, G (1998) *Farmers, Temples and Tombs*, Canongate, Edinburgh.

Boece, H (1527) *The History and Chronicles of Scotland*, (trans. John Bellenden).

Council for British Archaeology, York. Flint find points to Scotland's first people, *British Archaeology*, May/June 2009.

Burt, E (1754) *Letters from the North of Scotland*, intro. Withers, C (1998) Birlinn, Edinburgh.

Cowan, IB and Easson DE (1976) *Medieval Religious Houses*, Scotland, Longman, London.

Croft, WD (1961) *A New History of Scotland,* vol. 1, Nelson, Edinburgh.

Devine, TM (1994) *The Transformation of Rural Scotland: Social Change and the Agrarian Economy 1600–1815*, John Donald, Edinburgh.

Diamond, J (1999) *Guns, Germs and Steel*, Norton, New York.

Dixon, P (2002) *Puir Labourers and Busy Husbandmen*, Historic Scotland/Birlinn, Edinburgh.

Donkin, RA (1958) Cistercian sheep, farming and wool-sales in the thirteenth century, *Agricultural History Review*, vol. 6.

Driscoll, S (2002) *Alba, The Gaelic Kingdom of Scotland*, Historic Scotland/Birlinn, Edinburgh.

Duncan, AAM (1986) *Scotland: The Making of the Kingdom*, Mercat Press, Edinburgh.

Duncan, CAM, (1991) On identifying a sound environmental ethic in history, *Environmental History Review*, vol. 15.

Evans, JG (1975) *The Environment of Early Man in the British Isles*, Elek, London.

Fagan, B (2000) *The Little Ice Age*, Basic Books, New York.

Fenton, A (1999) *Scottish Country Life*, Tuckwell Press, East Lothian.

—(1963) Skene of Hallyard's manuscript 'On Husbandrie', *British Agricultural Review*, vol. 11.

Grant, IF (1961) *Highland Folk Ways*, Routledge and Kegan Paul Ltd, London.

Gillen, C (2003) *Geology and Landscapes in Scotland*, Terra Publishing, Hertfordshire.

Haldane, ARB (1952) *The Drove Roads of Scotland*, David and Charles, Devon.

—(1962) *New Ways through the Glens*, House of Lochar, Isle of Colonsay, Argyll.

Hall, D (2002) *Burgess, Merchant and Priest*, Historic Scotland/Birlinn, Edinburgh.

Herman, A (2001) *The Scottish Enlightenment*, Fourth Estate, London.

Hingley, R (1998) *Settlement and Sacrifice*, Canongate/Batsford, Edinburgh.

Hughes, JD (2001) *An Environmental History of the World*, Routledge, London and New York.

Hume, JR and Moss, MS (1981) *The Making of Scotch Whisky*, Canongate, Edinburgh.

Hume Brown, P (ed) (originally published in 1894) *Early Travellers in Scotland*, 1974, James Thin, Edinburgh.

Hunter, J (1976) *The Making of the Crofting Community*, John Donald, Edinburgh.

—(1999) *Last of the Free*, Mainstream, Edinburgh.

Lamb, HH (1982) *Climate History and the Modern World*, Methuen, London.

Love, J (2003) *Machair*, Scottish Natural Heritage, Perth.

Lynch, M (1992) *A New History of Scotland*, Pimlico, London.

(ed) (2001) *The Oxford Companion to Scottish History*, Oxford University Press.

Mabey, R (1996) *Flora Britannica*, Sinclair Stevenson, London.

Macdonald, MJ (1937) *Highland Ponies*, Eneas Mackay, Stirling.

McGregor, RK (1988) Deriving a biocentric history: evidence from the journal of Henry David Thoreau, *Environmental Review* 12.

Mackie, JD (1978) *A History of Scotland*, Penguin Books, London.

McNab, C (2004) *The Great Book of Guns*, Thunder Bay Press, San Diego, California.

Miller, J (1985) *A Portrat of Caithness and Sutherland*, Robert Hale, London.

(1994) *A Wild and Open Sea*, Orkney Press, Kirkwall.

Milliken, W and Bridgewater, S (2004) *Flora Celtica*, Birlinn, Edinburgh.

Morrison, A (1980) *Early Man in Britain and Ireland*, Croom Helm, London.

Nethersole Thompson, D and Watson, A (1974) *The Cairngorms*, Collins, London.

Orr, W (1982) *Deer Forests, Landlords and Crofters*, John Donald, Edinburgh.

Owen, O (1999) *The Sea Road: A Viking Voyage Through Scotland*, Historic Scotland/Canongate, Edinburgh.

Parry, ML and Slater, TR (eds) (1980) *The Making of the Scottish Countryside*, Croom Helm, London.

Pepper, D (1996) *Modern Environmentalism*, Routledge, London.

Phillips, R (1977) *Wild Flowers of Britain*, Pan Books, London.

Prebble, J (1961) *Culloden*, Secker and Warburg, London.

—(1963) *The Highland Clearances*, Secker and Warburg, London.

Price, RJ (1983) *Scotland's Environment During the Last 30,000 Years*, Scottish Academic Press, Edinburgh.

Pryde, GS (1962) *Scotland From 1603 to the Present Day*, Thomas Nelson and Sons, Edinburgh.

Rackham, O (1990) *Trees and Woodland in the British Landscape*, Phoenix Press, London.

Richards, E (2005) *The Highland Clearances*, Birlinn, Edinburgh.

Ritchie, J (1920) *The Influence of Man on Animal Life in Scotland*, Cambridge University Press.

Roberts, A (2006) *Tales of the Morar Highlands*, Birlinn, Edinburgh.

Ross, D (2001) *Scottish Place-names*, Birlinn, Edinburgh.

Schama, S (1995) *Landscape and Memory*, Harper Perennial, London.

Shaw, J (1984) *Water Power in Scotland 1550–1870*, John Donald, Edinburgh.

Shaw J, Stell, G and Storrier, S (eds) (2003) *Scottish Life and Society: A Compendium of Scottish Ethnology, Scotland's Buildings*, Tuckwell Press, East Linton.

Smout, TC (1993) *Scotland since Prehistory*, Scottish Cultural Press, Aberdeen.

—(1969) *A History of the Scottish People, 1560–1830*, Collins, London.

—(ed.) (2003) *People and Woods in Scotland*, Edinburgh University Press.

— Smout, TC and Fenton, (eds) (1965) Scottish agriculture before the Improvers: an exploration, *Agricultural History Review*, 13.

Tabraham, C (2005) *Scotland's Castles*, BT Batsford/Historic Scotland, London.

Turnock, D (1982) *The Historical Geography of Scotland since 1707*, CUP, Cambridge.

Warren, C (2002) *Managing Scotland's Environment*, Edinburgh University Press.

Watt, DER (ed) (1998) *A History Book for Scots: Selections From Walter Bower, Scotichronicon*, Mercat Press, Edinburgh.

Index

A

abbeys
  Dryburgh 117, 137
  Dundrennan 116
  Glenluce 116
  Jedburgh 76, 134, 138
  Kelso 71, 76, 117, 137, 138, 165
  Lindisfarne 136
  Lismore 25, 135
  Melrose 76, 117, 136, 137
  Tiree 135, 197
Aberdeenshire 17, 30, 37, 79, 105, 191, 196
Abernethy, Treaty of 130
Abernyte 154
acid deposition 169, 170
acid rain 170
industrial pollution 168, 169, 171
adzes 118
agate 32
Agricola, Gnaeus Julius 46
agriculture 48–51, 173–199
  beginnings in Scotland 35–44
  cash economy in 24, 83, 124, 145, 146, 148, 152, 181, 182, 187, 188, 193
  clearance for 48, 50, 53, 54
  commercialisation of 60, 62, 75, 78 81, 145, 146, 152
  concern for in 1690s 79, 147, 150, 151, 152, 154, 159
  conservatism in 156, 158, 184
  crop failure 62, 66, 74, 80, 150, 157, 173, 191
  disrupted by war 76, 170
  in Eastern Coastal Lowlands 24, 48, 56, 114, 115–16
  environmental impacts of 43–44, 48–51, 61–62, 114, 118, 131, 145, 153, 234
  failure of in 1780s 163
  and feudal government 62
  at Foulis 179–180
  Improved 151–56, 160–71, 173, 176, 177, 187–88
  innovations 24, 32, 35, 53, 61, 62, 93, 147–48, 180, 205
  Iron Age intensifications of 49
  in lowlands 48, 49, 57, 62, 102, 114, 115, 116, 124, 146–48, 153, 155, 157–61, 173, 180
  in the Medieval Warm Period 61–62, 68, 71–72, 101, 117, 205
  obliteration of Neolithic remains by 30
  products as rent 114, 124, 142, 148, 182, 185, 187
  regional profile of 60
  Roman influence on 24, 62, 110, 118
  transition from subsistence 164
  in uplands 85, 48, 50, 55, 56–57, 71, 78, 115, 118, 155, 175, 186
  Viking influence on 62 119
Ailsa Craig 12
Alaska 22
Alba 69, 70, 128, 213, 216
  defeats Vikings at the Battle of Strathearn 70
  first unified territory of 69
  thanage system in 128
Albert, Prince Consort 195
Alexander I 210
Alexander II 72, 110, 137, 210, 213
Alexander III 76, 134, 210
Alps 67

Notes from the North

Emma Wood

ISBN 1 84282 048 6 PBK £7.99

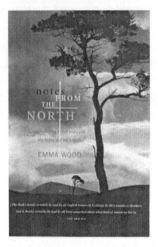

Notes from the North is a pragmatic, positive and forward-looking contribution to cultural and political debate within Scotland.

- Notes on being English
- Notes on being in Scotland
- Learning from a shared past

Sickened by the English jingoism that surfaced in rampant form during the 1982 Falklands War, Emma Wood started to dream of moving from her home in East Anglia to the Highlands of Scotland. She felt increasingly frustrated and marginalised as Thatcherism got a grip on the southern English psyche. The Scots she met on frequent holidays in the Highlands had no truck with Thatcherism, and she felt at home with grass-roots Scottish anti-authoritarianism. The decision was made. She uprooted and headed for a new life in the north of Scotland.

In this book she sets a study of Scots-English conflicts alongside relevant personal experiences of contemporary incomers' lives in the Highlands. She was to discover that she had crossed a border in more than the geographical sense. Her own approach has been thoughtful and creative.

This is an intelligent and perceptive book. It is calm, reflective, witty and sensitive about an issue which can sometimes generate more heat than light. ...it should...be read by all Scots concerned about what kind of nation we live in. They might learn something about themselves. THE HERALD

[Wood's] assimilation into Scotland caused her delight and despair, but her enlightenment is evident on every page of this perceptive, provocative book. MAIL ON SUNDAY

The Hydro Boys

Emma Wood

ISBN 1 84282 047 8 PBK £8.99

'I heard about drowned farms and hamlets, the ruination of the salmon-fishing and how Inverness might be washed away if the dams failed inland. I was told about the huge veins of crystal they found when they were tunneling deep under the mountains and when I wanted to know who "they" were: what stories I got in reply! I heard about Poles, Czechs, poverty-stricken Irish, German spies, intrepid locals and the heavy drinking, fighting and gambling which went on in the NOSHEB contractors' camps.'

The hydro-electric project was a crusade, with a marvellous goal: the prize of affordable power for all from Scottish rainfall.

This book is a journey through time, and across and beneath the Highland landscape... it is not just a story of technology and politics but of people.

Nobody should forget the human sacrifice made by those who built the dams all those years ago. The politicians, engineers and navvies of the era bequeathed to us the major source of renewable energy down to the present day. Their legacy will continue to serve us far into the 21st century. BRIAN WILSON MP, Energy Minister, THE SCOTSMAN

Luath Press Limited

committed to publishing well written books worth reading

LUATH PRESS takes its name from Robert Burns, whose little collie Luath (*Gael.*, swift or nimble) tripped up Jean Armour at a wedding and gave him the chance to speak to the woman who was to be his wife and the abiding love of his life. Burns called one of the 'Twa Dogs' Luath after Cuchullin's hunting dog in Ossian's *Fingal*.

Luath Press was established in 1981 in the heart of Burns country, and is now based a few steps up the road from Burns' first lodgings on Edinburgh's Royal Mile. Luath offers you distinctive writing with a hint of unexpected pleasures.

Most bookshops in the UK, the US, Canada, Australia, New Zealand and parts of Europe, either carry our books in stock or can order them for you. To order direct from us, please send a £sterling cheque, postal order, international money order or your credit card details (number, address of cardholder and expiry date) to us at the address below. Please add post and packing as follows: UK – £1.00 per delivery address; overseas surface mail – £2.50 per delivery address; overseas airmail – £3.50 for the first book to each delivery address, plus £1.00 for each additional book by airmail to the same address. If your order is a gift, we will happily enclose your card or message at no extra charge.

Luath Press Limited
543/2 Castlehill
The Royal Mile
Edinburgh EH1 2ND
Scotland
Telephone: +44 (0)131 225 4326 (24 hours)
Fax: +44 (0)131 225 4324
email: sales@luath. co.uk
Website: www. luath.co.uk